risotto

risotto

hamlyn

First published in 2002
by Hamlyn
a division of Octopus Publishing Group Ltd
2–4 Heron Quays, London E14 4JP

Copyright © 2002 Octopus Publishing Group Ltd

ISBN 0 600 60646 5

A CIP catalogue record for this book is available in the British Library

Printed and bound in China

10 9 8 7 6 5 4 3 2 1

NOTES

1 The Department of Health advises that eggs should not be consumed raw. This book contains some dishes made with raw or lightly cooked eggs. It is prudent for more vulnerable people such as pregnant and nursing mothers, invalids, the elderly, babies and young children to avoid uncooked or lightly cooked dishes made with eggs.

2 Meat and poultry should be cooked thoroughly. Keep refrigerated until ready for cooking. To test if poultry is cooked, pierce the flesh through the thickest part with a skewer or fork – the juices should run clear, never pink or red.

3 This book includes dishes made with nuts and nut derivatives. It is advisable for those with known allergic reactions to nuts and nut derivatives and those who may be potentially vulnerable to these allergies, such as pregnant and nursing mothers, invalids, the elderly, babies, and children, to avoid dishes made with nuts and nut oils. It is also prudent to check the labels of preprepared ingredients for the possible inclusion of nut derivatives.

Contents

Introduction

Rice is to northern Italy what pasta is to the southern regions – it's the most widely used and popular staple food. It appears on lunch and dining tables as an accompaniment or as a course in its own right, unless soup is being served first. But every Italian is a born gourmet and no one would dream of serving food on a bed of plain, boiled rice, no matter how rich and elaborate the main dish.

Accordingly, Italian cooks invented risotto – literally meaning 'little rice'. Risottos, or more correctly *risotti*, may be simply flavoured with herbs, spices, a little cheese, tomatoes or other vegetables or they can be rich and elaborate combinations of meat, fish, shellfish, chicken, vegetables, cream, cheese, mushrooms and dozens of other ingredients. What they all have in common is the unique creamy texture of the rice and a perfect balance of aromas and flavours.

What is risotto?

It is probably easier to define what risotto is not rather than what it is. It is not simply any old mixture of rice and other ingredients and it is never made from leftovers. It is fundamentally a savoury rice dish, carefully flavoured with other ingredients – sometimes only one or two, sometimes more – cooked in a very specific way so that the flavours combine and meld. It takes time, care and an intuitive ability to 'feel' how the dish is developing as it cooks to make the perfect risotto. Both the technique (see page 14) and the type of rice (see page 10) are crucial to its success. Risotto's origins lie in the honourable tradition of peasant cookery, but this is far from saying it is an easy dish to perfect. On the contrary, an Italian cook will be judged by the quality of his or her risotto and it takes practice to match the standard.

Frugal cooks developed the idea of frying little risotto balls or cakes to use up leftover risotto and these have now become dishes in their own right. The popular appetizer *Arancini*, risotto balls filled with mozzarella cheese and then deep-fried, is actually a Sicilian recipe, but it has been enthusiastically adopted by the north, where it is known as *Supplì al Telefono*, telephone wires.

Italians also use rice for desserts and sweet dishes. While rice tarts and cakes are more popular, risotto-style rice puddings are quite frequently made.

Risotto – history and tradition

It is impossible to say when or by whom risotto was created and the great cities of the north – among them Milan, Venice, Bologna and Verona, as well as Rome – all claim to be its birthplace. The dish was certainly known in Milan in the sixteenth century. Italy's cuisine is one of the most venerable in Europe, tracing its origins back through ancient Rome to classical Greece and beyond. Alexander the Great invaded India in 326 BC and his army is known to have brought rice back with them to Europe. Much later, in the eleventh century, the Crusaders and their enemies the Saracens also imported rice from the Middle East. The round grain rice used for risotto first appeared in Italy in the fifteenth century and its cultivation was fostered by the powerful Sforza Dukes of Milan. Certainly, rice is a long-established European staple and has been successfullly cultivated in the Po valley since the sixteenth century. Italian rice became so famous that its export was banned by law. Even so, Thomas Jefferson, founding father of the American constitution and the republic's third president, smuggled two sacks of Italian rice out of the Piedmont back to his home in Virginia to cultivate on his estate. Italy remains today the largest producer of rice in Europe.

To understand how this humble, rather bland grain became transformed into one of the world's most famous and popular dishes means learning how Italians feel about cooking and food in general. Eating, especially with all the family gathered together, is regarded as one of life's great pleasures. Even in today's busy world, a relaxed two- or three-hour weekend lunch with several generations of aunts and

uncles, cousins, nephews and nieces, grandparents and babies is still the social high point of many Italian calendars, although it may no longer be a weekly event. While catching up with each other's news and laughing and joking are an integral part of it, the meal itself lies at the heart of the occasion and the quality must be impeccable. Time spent at the market and in the kitchen is regarded as well spent and each dish is savoured and appreciated by all the diners. For Italians, choosing ingredients and cooking them are acts of love and never a chore.

Almost more than any other cuisine in the world, Italian cooking is based around the seasons. Fruit and vegetables in particular are used at their youngest and freshest, but care is also taken that fish, cheese, meat, poultry and herbs are in peak condition before they are even offered for sale. Although modern transport means that most produce can be available almost anywhere in the world at any time of year, there is still a strong tradition, especially outside large cities, of using foods in season. This, in turn, generates an understanding of which ingredients have a natural affinity with each other and which combinations work best. Seafood, for example, is never served with cheese, as the flavours are not considered complementary and the mixture is indigestible. The tendency of foreigners to sprinkle quantities of grated Parmesan over every risotto served to them,

including mussel, squid, prawn and clam, evokes expressions of horror and outrage on the faces of any Italian observers.

Risotto was born out of this combination of a joyous delight in preparing and cooking food and a seasonal approach to ingredients. To serve plain rice would indicate a lack of care and interest in the food and, by implication, in the people who were to eat it. Perhaps the first risotto simply consisted of rice, cooked in stock to add flavour, with butter and cheese stirred in, for this northern region is also dairy farming country. From here, it was a small step to the inclusion of sun-ripened tomatoes, lightly sautéed fennel, freshly caught mussels or succulent Parma ham.

Italian cooking, even today, is distinctly regional and, in some cases, even local. For centuries cooks have perfected their local specialities, passing the recipes down the generations. Classic risottos all feature ingredients characteristic of northern Italy – butter, rather than olive oil, freshwater and sea fish, highly seasoned sausages and salami, Gorgonzola and Parmesan cheese, game, asparagus, herbs, mushrooms and truffles. Rivalry between the regions is intense, with both Lombardy and the Veneto claiming 'ownership' of more than fifty classic risotto recipes. The Veneto is famous for its seafood risottos and is also home to *Risi e Bisi*, a risotto made with

fresh green peas that was always served at the Doge's annual St Mark's banquet in Venice. Golden-coloured, saffron-flavoured *Risotto alla Milanese* or *Risotto Giallo* is probably the best-known risotto in the world and Lombardy also boasts a superb and unusual lemon risotto. The Piedmont transforms a simple *Risotto Bianco* (see page 14) – rice, shallots, Parmesan cheese and butter – into a gourmet dish by grating fragrant, locally grown white truffles on top.

It was at the comparatively late date of 1861 that Italy became a unified state, but cooking, as with many other important aspects of Italian daily life, remained firmly based in the regions. An invisible culinary frontier continued to separate the north from the south, which was eventually breached by the Tuscans. Gradually an interchange of ingredients, techniques and dishes took place and today rice is served throughout the south and pasta has found its way to the north. Risotto is now known throughout the world and a new generation of chefs has created exotic recipes that are a far cry from the simple peasant dish, based on fresh local produce, that it once was. Yet even these risottos with lobster, mangoes, soy sauce or vodka are true to the traditional technique and prepared with the same devoted attention.

Essential Ingredients

Risotto rice

Italian rice is a medium grain that is larger than round-grain or pudding rice and rounder than long-grain rice. There are four sub-categories of Italian rice: semifino is best used in soups; ordinario is ideal for puddings, rice tarts and cakes, while fino and superfino are used for risottos. Generally speaking, the better the quality of the rice, the longer the cooking time. Superfino requires about 20 minutes, while ordinario needs only about 12 minutes. Probably the best-known superfino rice is arborio, which is extensively farmed and widely exported. Other superfino varieties include Carnaroli, Roma and Maratelli. A useful fino, which has slightly longer grains than superfino, is Vialone Nano. Sometimes packets are just labelled 'risotto rice', but it is worth keeping an eye open for these specific varieties.

The secret of risotto rice lies in the capacity of the grains to absorb very large quantities of liquid, whether wine, stock or water, swelling to about three times their original size without becoming soggy. The rice cooks to a wonderful creamy texture, but at the same retains firmness and 'bite'. Like pasta, it is cooked until it is 'al dente' – to the tooth. Unlike some other types of rice, risotto rice should never be rinsed before cooking, as this washes away the starch – a self-defeating act because the high starch content is what creates the special texture. Easy-cook risotto rice is also available, but it does not produce the authentic creaminess characteristic of the dish and is hardly any more convenient to use than standard risotto rice.

Store rice in a sealed container in a cool, dry place. It will keep for several months.

The first rule for making a perfect risotto is to use a fino or superfino rice. You can produce a passable risotto-style dish with long-grain rice, but it will not have the same texture and is liable to stick to the bottom of the saucepan.

Tomatoes

Like any dish, risotto is only as good as the quality of the original ingredients. Whatever these are, they should be as fresh as possible. This is particularly true of vegetables. If you are using fresh tomatoes, try to obtain sun-ripened ones, which have a sweeter, fuller flavour than those grown under glass. Vine tomatoes are usually sun-ripened, but more expensive. Plum tomatoes, a classic Italian ingredient, are less watery than many other varieties.

Herbs

Fresh herbs are always preferable to dried. If you cannot obtain fresh ones, look for freeze-dried herbs, which often have a better flavour, colour and texture than conventionally dried ones. If you are substituting dried herbs for fresh, use only a third of the quantity. Italian parsley is the flat leaf variety. Do not chop basil, as the delicate leaves are easily bruised. Tear it into small pieces instead.

Spices

As a rule, few spices are featured in risottos, but two – chillies and saffron – do play important roles. Dried red chillies, known as *peperoncini*, are a speciality of the Abruzzi. They are extremely fiery and nicknamed *diavoletti*, little devils. Saffron plays the starring role in the classic Risotto alla Milanese (see page 92) and is widely used in seafood risottos. It has a special affinity with mussels. It is the world's most expensive spice – at one time stealing it was a capital offence in Italy – but there is no substitute. Be wary about buying cheaper saffron, which may turn out to be safflower. It is similar in appearance, but paler than the orange-red saffron and, although it adds colour to risotto, it will not add flavour. Fortunately, only a small quantity of saffron is required. Crush the threads and infuse them in water or stock before adding to the dish. Saffron powder is also available, but this may be adulterated with safflower.

Cheese

Many risottos call for grated Parmesan cheese. It is best to buy this in a block and grate it freshly when it is required, rather than using ready grated Parmesan, which quickly becomes tasteless. Look for Parmesan with Parmigiano Reggiano stamped on the rind, which means that it comes from a strictly defined area between Parma and Modena and is a guarantee of quality. If you buy it from a delicatessen or specialist cheese shop, a wedge will be freshly cut from the cheese wheel and this will have a better flavour and texture than pre-packed cheese. It can be stored, wrapped in foil or muslin, in the refrigerator for at least a month. Other Italian cheeses you may need include mozzarella, fontina, mascarpone and Gorgonzola. The best mozzarella, di bufala, is made from water buffalo milk. Fontina is creamy cheese produced in the Val d'Aosta in the Italian Alps. Mascarpone is very rich, triple-cream cheese from Lombardy and Gorgonzola is one of the world's great veined cheeses. It was once produced in the village of Gorgonzola – the cheese's full name is Stracchino Gorgonzola – now subsumed by suburban Milan and is today made throughout Lombardy. Butter is essential for making risotto. Italians always cook with unsalted butter and this is generally best for risottos. However, you can use salted butter for most of the recipes in this book if you prefer, except where unsalted is particularly specified because salted butter would spoil the flavour of the dish.

Olive oil

There is no substitute for olive oil, which has a distinctive flavour. In fact, olive oils from different regions of Italy, let alone from other countries, have individual flavours. The most widely acclaimed Italian olive oils are from Liguria and Apulia. Extra virgin is the best quality and most expensive. It is made from the first cold pressing of olives and has a maximum acidity of 1 per cent. Virgin olive oil, which may be sub-divided into superfine, fine and virgin, is also cold pressed and low in acidity. Anything simply labelled 'pure olive oil' is refined oil that has probably been heat treated. It lacks character and flavour and is not worth buying. Light olive oil, produced from the last cold pressing, has a very mild flavour. Estate oils are the equivalent of château wines. They are made from olives grown on a single estate, usually hand-picked and pressed almost immediately. They are very fine, extremely expensive and best reserved for salad dressings. The colour of olive oil is no indication of its flavour or quality.

Lemons

It is best to buy unwaxed lemons if you need to grate the rind. Lemons are often treated with an ethylene gas to preserve their colour and keep the skins looking fresh. When squeezing fruit for juice, first roll it over the work surface several times to increase the yield.

Mushrooms

Italians are enthusiastic gatherers of mushrooms, so wild mushrooms feature in many risotto recipes. If you are going to pick your own, you must be absolutely certain that you can identify them accurately (in Italy, most helpfully, the local pharmacy will most helpfully do this for you). Some poisonous fungi look very similar to edible varieties. Most supermarkets now stock a range of wild mushrooms, although this is something of a misnomer as many of these species are now cultivated. Nevertheless, they do have more flavour than the common cultivated mushroom. Never wash mushrooms, as they absorb water like a sponge and become soggy. Simply brush them gently or wipe with damp kitchen paper. Porcini mushrooms, also known as ceps, are an especial favourite. They are available dried from both supermarkets and Italian delicatessens. Although they are expensive, you need use only a very small quantity, as they have a strong flavour, accentuated by drying. To reconstitute dried porcini, place them in a small bowl and pour in enough hot water to cover. Set aside for about 20 minutes, until soft. Drain and use like fresh mushrooms. Reserve the soaking water, which has a concentrated mushroom flavour, and use as stock.

Most of the ingredients used in the recipes in this book are widely available

from supermarkets. An Italian delicatessen would be a good place to buy any speciality ingredients, such as pancetta, Italian cheeses and olive paste. You can also make olive paste yourself very easily by processing 500 g/1 lb pitted black olives in a food processor while adding 5–6 tablespoons extra virgin olive oil through the feeder tube.

The importance of stock

Good quality light stock is essential for making risotto. Chicken and vegetable stock are most commonly used. Fish or shellfish stock give seafood risottos a wonderful flavour, but vegetable stock can be substituted. A light beef stock is used more rarely, but pork, lamb and bacon stock are all too strong. (See pages 16–19 for stock recipes.)

Home-made stock is flavoursome, you know exactly what has gone into it and you can skim off the fat, so it is healthy too. It is not difficult to make, although some types do require long cooking. Make a big batch of stock to save time and freeze it in portions for future use.

If home-made stock is not available, you can use stock cubes or bouillon powder. It is worth spending the extra money on good quality brands and checking the labels before buying. Some stock cubes contain monosodium glutamate and many are very high in salt.

When cooking risottos, always heat the stock in a separate pan to simmering point before adding it to the rice. Keep the stock at a gentle simmer throughout the process.

Equipment

You will need a large saucepan, with a lid, that can contain the rice once it has finished cooking, bearing in mind that the grains will swell to about three times their original size. It should be heavy-based – cast iron, copper or heavy-gauge steel or aluminium – to prevent the risotto from sticking and burning. A nonstick pan is of no particular advantage. A pan with a curved or rounded base is ideal as it prevents the rice from sticking around the edge of the base. Some risottos in this book are cooked in a frying pan. Again, this should be large and heavy-based.

The stock is added to rice a ladleful at a time, so a soup ladle is essential. Most hold 125–150 ml/4–5 fl oz. A wooden or plastic handle is safer than a metal one, as you are more than likely to leave the ladle resting in the pan of hot stock while you are cooking.

Any other equipment required for cooking risotto is likely to be found in most kitchens already – a measuring jug and spoons, chopping board and knives, a grater and a wooden spoon. A food processor is useful, but not essential.

How to make the perfect risotto

All risottos are made in basically the same way. Risotto should be prepared immediately before serving, although there is a trick for partially cooking in advance (see below). The following recipe is a basic risotto with Parmesan, which illustrates the general technique for all risottos.

Risotto bianco

1–1.2 litres/1¾–2 pints Vegetable Stock
  (see page 19)
50 g/2 oz butter, preferably unsalted
2 shallots, finely chopped
300 g/10 oz risotto rice
5 tablespoons dry white wine
40 g/1½ oz Parmesan cheese,
  freshly grated
salt

1. Bring the stock to simmering point in a large pan. The recipes in this book always specify precisely the quantity of stock. However, different varieties of risotto rice may absorb slightly more or less stock, so it is sensible to bring a little more than the specified amount to simmering point. Then, if you do need more stock, it is already hot. Note that, in the recipes, the stock is almost invariably listed in the ingredients as 'hot stock' and this step does not then appear in the method.

Step-by-Step Risotto

2. Melt half the butter in a large, heavy-based pan over a low heat. (Some recipes specify butter, some olive oil and others a mixture of the two.) Add the shallots (most savoury risottos include at least one member of the onion family) and sauté gently. Cook them over a low heat, stirring occasionally, for about 5 minutes, until softened and translucent, but not coloured. It is important that the onion is properly softened at this stage because although it will continue to cook, it will not soften further once the rice has been added. A tip is to add a pinch of salt when you start to sauté the onion, this will release the moisture and will prevent it from cooking too quickly.

3. Add the rice to the pan and stir constantly with a wooden spoon over a low heat for 1–2 minutes, until all the grains are coated with butter and have become translucent. At this point they will be beginning to stick to the base of the pan.

4. Pour in the wine and bring to the boil over a medium heat, stirring constantly. Cook, stirring constantly, until almost all the liquid has evaporated. (Not every recipe includes wine and in some recipes it is simply heated with the stock.)

5. Add a ladleful of the simmering stock and cook over a medium heat, stirring constantly, until it has been completely absorbed by the rice. Continue adding the stock, 1 ladleful at a time, and continue cooking and stirring. Make sure that each addition of stock has been completely absorbed before you add any more. The liquid should be at a fairly vigorous simmer, so adjust the heat if necessary. Until you feel confident about making risottos, it is sensible to stir constantly throughout the cooking process. However, once you are more familiar with the 'feel' of the rice, you can stir constantly to begin with and then only frequently after about 10 minutes. The purpose of stirring is to release the starch, as well as to prevent the rice from sticking to the base of pan, although Italian cooks will tell you that a perfect risotto just catches on the base. You may need to add a little more stock than specified in the recipes if the mixture becomes dry (see step 1). It will take about 20 minutes for the rice to cook. The grains should be plump and tender, but still firm, and the texture should be creamy.

6. Remove the pan from the heat and stir in the remaining butter and the Parmesan. This is called the *mantecatura*.

Cover the pan and leave the risotto to rest for 2–3 minutes. During this time, the butter and Parmesan will melt. Remove the lid and stir vigorously to increase the creaminess and serve immediately.

Part cooking risotto in advance

Ideally, risotto should always be made just before it is to be served, but as it requires constant attention, it can be frustrating when you are entertaining unless your guests are happy to keep you company in the kitchen. The technique described below is quite a successful way of cheating.

Prepare the risotto up to the point where you have sautéed the rice and the grains are well coated in butter or oil. Add 2 ladlefuls of hot stock and, when it has returned to the boil, cover the pan tightly and turn off the heat. If necessary for a firm seal, wrap a tea towel around the saucepan lid first. When you are ready to resume cooking, the rice will have absorbed all the stock and will be half cooked. Stir in a knob of butter and continue adding stock, 1 ladleful at a time, stirring constantly over a medium heat. The rice will take about 10 minutes more to cook.

Stocks

Makes about 1.5 litres/2½ pints/ Preparation time: 10 minutes, plus cooling/ Cooking time: 35 minutes

Fish Stock

1. Put the fish heads, bones and trimmings in a large saucepan and add the onion, carrot, celery, herbs and peppercorns. Pour in the wine and water.

2. Bring to the boil, cover and simmer over a low heat for 30 minutes.

3. Remove the pan from the heat and strain. Cover, leave to cool, then store in the refrigerator until required or freeze.

1 kg/2 lb heads, bones and trimmings of white fish,
   rinsed in cold water

1 onion, finely chopped

1 carrot, thinly sliced

1 celery stick, thinly sliced

6 parsley sprigs

1 thyme sprig

1 fennel sprig

6 black peppercorns

150 ml/¼ pint dry white wine

1.8 litres/3 pints water

Makes about 2.5 litres/4 pints/ Preparation time: 15 minutes, plus chilling/ Cooking time: 3½ hours

Chicken Stock

1.3 kg/3 lb chicken wings and necks

2 onions, cut into wedges

4 litres/7 pints water

2 carrots, chopped

2 celery sticks, chopped

10 parsley sprigs

2 thyme sprigs

2 bay leaves

10 black peppercorns

1. Put the chicken wings and necks and the onions in a large, heavy-based saucepan. Cook over a low heat, stirring frequently, until lightly browned all over.
2. Add the water and bring to the boil, scraping up any sediment from the base of the pan with a wooden spoon. Skim off the scum that rises to the surface. Add the carrots, celery, parsley, thyme, bay leaves and peppercorns, partially cover and simmer gently for 3 hours.
3. Remove the pan from the heat and strain the stock. Cover, leave to cool, then chill in the refrigerator overnight. Remove and discard the layer of fat that will have set on the surface.

Stocks

Makes about 2 litres/3½ pints/ Preparation time: 20 minutes, plus chilling/ Cooking time: 5¼ hours

Beef Stock

1.75 kg/3½ lb beef bones, chopped into
    7 cm/3 inch pieces

2 onions, quartered

2 carrots, chopped

2 celery sticks, chopped

2 tomatoes, chopped

4 litres/7 pints water

10 parsley sprigs

4 thyme sprigs

2 bay leaves

8 black peppercorns

1. Put the beef bones into a large roasting tin and roast in a preheated oven, 230°C (450°F), Gas Mark 8, for 30 minutes, until lightly browned. Turn the bones occasionally during cooking. Add the onions, carrots, celery and tomatoes, spoon over the fat in the tin and roast, stirring occasionally, for a further 30 minutes.

2. Using a slotted spoon, transfer the bones and vegetables to a large saucepan. Drain off the fat from the roasting tin and add 150 ml/¼ pint of the water. Set the roasting tin over a low heat and bring to the boil, scraping up any sediment from the base of the pan. Pour this into the saucepan and add the remaining water.

3. Bring to the boil, skimming off the scum that rises to the surface. Add the parsley, thyme, bay leaves and peppercorns. Partially cover the pan, lower the heat and simmer for 4 hours.

4. Strain the stock, cover and leave to cool. Chill in the refrigerator overnight, then remove and discard the layer of fat that will have set on the surface.

**Makes about 600 ml/1 pint/ Preparation time: 5 minutes, plus cooling/
Cooking time: 30 minutes**

Vegetable Stock

50 g/2 oz butter

2 onions, chopped

2 leeks, thinly sliced

2 carrots, chopped

2 celery sticks, chopped

1 fennel bulb, chopped

1 thyme sprig

1 marjoram sprig

1 fennel sprig

4 parsley sprigs

900 ml/1½ pints water

1. Melt the butter in a large heavy-based saucepan. Add the onions, leeks, carrots, celery and fennel, stir well to coat, then cover and cook over a low heat for 10 minutes.
2. Stir in the herbs and add the water. Bring to the boil, cover and simmer for 15 minutes.
3. Remove the pan from the heat and strain. Cover, leave to cool, then store in the refrigerator until required or freeze.

1 Vegetables

Serves 4/ Preparation time: 10 minutes/ Cooking time: 25 minutes

Green Vegetable Risotto

A quick and easy risotto, this is the perfect choice if you are making a risotto for the first time.

125 g/4 oz butter

1 tablespoon olive oil

1 garlic clove, crushed and chopped

1 onion, finely diced

300 g/10 oz risotto rice

1 litre/1¾ pints hot Chicken or Vegetable Stock
  (see pages 17 and 19)

125 g/4 oz French beans, topped and tailed and
  cut into 2.5 cm/1 inch pieces

125 g/4 oz shelled peas

125 g/4 oz shelled and skinned broad beans

125 g/4 oz asparagus, topped and tailed and cut
  in to 2.5 cm/1 inch pieces

125 g/4 oz baby spinach, washed and chopped

75 ml/3 fl oz dry vermouth or white wine

2 tablespoons chopped parsley

125 g/4 oz Parmesan cheese, freshly grated

salt and pepper

1. Melt 50 g/2 oz of the butter with the olive oil in a heavy-based saucepan. Add the garlic and onion and sauté gently for 5 minutes, but do not allow to brown.

2. Add the rice and stir well to coat the grains with the butter and oil. Add the hot stock, a large ladleful at a time, stirring until each addition is absorbed into the rice. Continue adding stock in this way, cooking until the rice is creamy but the grains are still firm. This should take about 20 minutes.

3. When you add the last of the stock, add the vegetables and vermouth or white wine, mix well and cook for 2 minutes.

4. Remove the pan from the heat, season with salt and pepper and add the remaining butter, the chopped parsley and Parmesan. Mix well, then cover and leave the risotto to rest for a few minutes before serving.

Serves 4/ Preparation time: 10 minutes/ Cooking time: 30 minutes

Spring Greens and Goats' Cheese Risotto

4 tablespoons extra virgin olive oil

2 leeks, sliced

2 garlic cloves, chopped

250 g/8 oz risotto rice

150 ml/¼ pint dry white wine

1.2 litres/2 pints hot Vegetable Stock
(see page 19)

250 g/8 oz broccoli, cut into florets

250 g/8 oz baby spinach, shredded

25 g/1 oz chopped mixed herbs (such as basil,
chives, mint, parsley and tarragon)

125 g/4 oz soft goats' cheese, mashed

50 g/2 oz Parmesan cheese, freshly grated

salt and pepper

1. Heat the oil in a large saucepan and sauté the leeks and garlic for 5 minutes, until softened. Add the rice and stir well to coat the grains with the oil. Add the wine, bring to the boil and cook, stirring, until almost all the liquid has evaporated.

2. Add the hot stock, a ladleful at a time, stirring until each addition has been absorbed into the rice. Continue adding the stock in this way, cooking until the rice is creamy but the grains are still firm. This should take about 20 minutes. Add the broccoli to the rice after 12 minutes.

3. Stir the spinach, herbs and both cheeses into the rice. Season to taste with salt and pepper and cook for a final 2 minutes until the spinach is wilted. Cover the pan and leave the risotto to rest for a few minutes before serving.

Broad Bean, Lemon and Parmesan Risotto

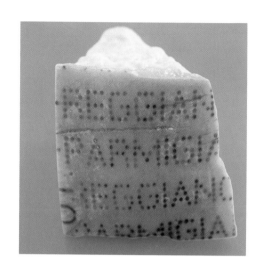

This is a wonderfully fragrant dish that is lovely when broad beans are first in season.

25 g/1 oz butter

2 tablespoons olive oil

1 onion, chopped

2 garlic cloves, crushed

400 g/13 oz risotto rice

150 ml/¼ pint dry white wine

1.2 litres/2 pints hot Vegetable Stock
   (see page 19)

150 g/5 oz fresh or frozen broad beans

50 g/2 oz Parmesan cheese, freshly grated, plus
   extra to serve

finely grated rind and juice of 1 lemon

salt and pepper

thyme sprigs, to garnish

1. Melt the butter with the oil in a large, heavy-based saucepan. Add the onion and garlic and sauté gently for 5 minutes until softened but not coloured. Add the rice and stir well to coat the grains with the butter and oil.

2. Add the wine, bring to the boil and cook, stirring, until almost all the liquid has evaporated. Add the hot stock, a ladleful at a time, stirring until each addition is absorbed into the rice. Continue adding stock in this way, until half the stock has been used. Stir in the beans.

3. Gradually add the remaining stock, a ladleful at a time as before, cooking until the rice is creamy but the grains are still firm. This will take about 20 minutes in total. Stir in the Parmesan, lemon rind and juice and season to taste with salt and pepper. Cover the pan and leave the risotto to rest for a few minutes before serving with extra Parmesan and thyme sprigs.

Serves 4/ Preparation time: 5–10 minutes/ Cooking time: 30 minutes

Country-style Risotto

Known as *risotto alla rustica*, this simple dish is packed with flavour.

2 tablespoons olive oil

40 g/1½ oz butter

2 shallots, finely chopped

1 small onion, finely chopped

1 rosemary sprig, finely chopped

1 tablespoon finely chopped parsley

¼ teaspoon finely chopped marjoram

4 basil leaves, finely chopped

1 garlic clove, crushed

375 g/12 oz risotto rice

50 ml/2 fl oz dry white wine

4 plum tomatoes, skinned

900 ml/1½ pints hot Vegetable Stock
   (see page 19)

2 tablespoons single cream

salt and pepper

1. Heat the oil and all but 1 teaspoon of the butter in a large heavy-based saucepan over a low heat. Add the shallots, onions, herbs and garlic and cook over a medium heat, stirring occasionally, for 5 minutes.
2. Add the rice, stir well to coat the grains with the butter and oil. Pour in the wine, bring to the boil and cook, stirring, until almost all the liquid has evaporated. Add the tomatoes, mashing with a fork. Mix thoroughly.
3. Add the hot stock, a large ladleful at a time, stirring until each addition is absorbed into the rice. Continue adding stock in this way, cooking until the rice is creamy but the grains are still firm. This should take about 20 minutes.
4. As the rice becomes creamy, add the reserved butter and plenty of pepper. Stir in the cream just before serving.

Lemon, Leek and Bay Leaf Risotto

The addition of bay to this lemon risotto imparts a wonderful flavour and aroma. This dish is a good accompaniment to grilled fish or shellfish.

50 g/2 oz butter

1 onion, finely chopped

2 garlic cloves, crushed

2 leeks, topped and tailed, washed and sliced

250 g/8 oz risotto rice

6 bay leaves, bruised

150 ml/¼ pint dry vermouth

1–1.2 litres/1¾–2 pints hot Chicken Stock or
  Vegetable Stock (see pages 17 and 19)

juice and rind of 1 large lemon

50 g/2 oz mascarpone cheese

50 g/2 oz Parmesan cheese, freshly grated, plus
  extra for serving

salt and pepper

1. Melt the butter in a heavy-based saucepan. Add the onion, garlic and leeks and sauté for 10 minutes, until softened but not browned. Add the rice and bay leaves and stir well to coat the grains with the butter. Add the vermouth, bring to the boil and cook until the liquid has reduced by half.

2. Add the hot stock, a ladleful at a time, stirring until each addition is absorbed into the rice. Continue adding stock in this way, cooking until the rice is creamy but the grains are still firm. This should take about 20 minutes.

3. Add the lemon juice and rind, season to taste with salt and pepper and stir for a further 5 minutes. Add the mascarpone and Parmesan, stir once, cover and leave the risotto to rest for a few minutes before serving with grated Parmesan.

Lemon and Thyme Risotto with Vodka

A wonderfully light and fragrant risotto. Serve on its own or as an accompaniment to a meat or fish dish.

125 g/4 oz butter

6 spring onions or young shallots, finely chopped

150 ml/¼ pint dry white wine

finely grated rind and juice of 1 large lemon

500 g/1 lb risotto rice

1.5 litres/2½ pints hot Chicken or Vegetable Stock (see pages 17 and 19)

2 tablespoons vodka

1 tablespoon chopped thyme

75 g/3 oz Parmesan cheese, freshly grated

salt and pepper

TO GARNISH:

thyme sprigs

strips of lemon rind

1. Melt half of the butter in a large heavy-based saucepan, add the spring onions or shallots and sauté for 5 minutes, until soft. Pour in the wine, add half the lemon rind, bring to the boil and cook, stirring, until almost all the liquid has evaporated.

2. Add the rice and stir well to coat the grains with the butter. Add the hot stock, a large ladleful at a time, stirring until each addition is absorbed into the rice. Continue adding stock in this way, cooking until the rice is creamy, but the grains are still firm. This should take about 20 minutes. Season to taste with salt and pepper. Stir in the remaining butter and lemon rind, the lemon juice, vodka, thyme and Parmesan.

3. Cover the pan and leave the risotto to rest for a few minutes before serving, garnished with thyme sprigs and strips of lemon rind.

Roasted Garlic and Leek Risotto

The garlic-infused oil adds an intense aroma and flavour to the risotto, while the deep-fried leeks give it an attractive appearance, making this an ideal dish to serve to guests.

6 large garlic cloves

about 150 ml/¼ pint olive oil

500 g/1 lb medium leeks, plus 2 extra to garnish

vegetable oil, for deep-frying

500 g/1 lb risotto rice

1.5 litres/2½ pints hot Chicken or Vegetable
   Stock (see pages 17 and 19)

50 g/2 oz Parmesan cheese, freshly grated

salt and pepper

1. Put the garlic cloves into a small saucepan. Cover completely with the olive oil and bring to a simmer. Simmer gently for about 20 minutes, or until the garlic is golden and soft. Leave the garlic to cool in the oil. Remove the garlic cloves once cool and set aside.

2. Meanwhile cut the 2 leeks for the garnish into 7 cm/3 inch lengths, then slice them in half lengthways and cut into long thin shreds. Deep-fry the shredded leeks for 1–2 minutes until crisp and just golden. Lift them out of the oil with a slotted spoon and drain on kitchen paper. Slice the remaining leeks.

3. Heat 75 ml/3 fl oz of the garlic-flavoured olive oil in a heavy-based saucepan. Add the sliced leeks and sauté for a few minutes until they are beginning to soften and colour slightly, then stir in the reserved garlic cloves.

4. Add the rice and stir well to coat the grains with the oil. Add the stock, a large ladleful at a time, stirring until each addition is absorbed into the rice. Continue adding stock in this way, cooking until the rice is creamy, but the grains are still firm. This should take about 20 minutes. Season well, stir in the Parmesan and cover the pan. Leave the risotto to rest for a few minutes before serving, garnished with a tangle of fried leeks.

Pumpkin, Sage and Chilli Risotto

125 g/4 oz butter

1 large onion, finely chopped

1–2 fresh or dried red chillies, deseeded and finely chopped

500 g/1 lb pumpkin, peeled and roughly chopped

500 g/1 lb risotto rice

1.5 litres/2½ pints hot Chicken or Vegetable Stock (see pages 17 and 19)

3 tablespoons chopped sage

75 g/3 oz Parmesan cheese, freshly grated

salt and pepper

sage sprigs, to garnish

1. Heat half the butter in a large saucepan and add the onion. Sauté over a low heat for 5 minutes until softened but not coloured. Stir in the chillies and cook for 1 minute. Add the pumpkin and cook, stirring constantly, for 5 minutes.

2. Add the rice and stir well to coat the grains with the butter. Add the hot stock, a large ladleful at a time, stirring until each addition is absorbed into the rice. Continue adding stock in this way, cooking until the rice is creamy but the grains are still firm. This should take about 20 minutes and the pumpkin should start to disintegrate. Season to taste with salt and pepper, then stir in the sage, the remaining butter and the Parmesan. Cover the pan and leave the risotto to rest for a few minutes before serving, garnished with sage sprigs.

Serves 4/ Preparation time: 10 minutes/ Cooking time: 45 minutes

Butternut Squash Risotto

1 butternut squash, weighing 1 kg/2 lb

3 tablespoons olive oil

125 g/4 oz butter

1 garlic clove, finely chopped

1 onion, finely diced

300 g/10 oz risotto rice

1 litre/1¾ pints hot Chicken or Vegetable stock
  (see pages 17 and 19)

150 g/5 oz Parmesan cheese, freshly grated

salt and pepper

pumpkin seed oil, to serve

1. Top and tail the squash, cut it around the middle, then pare away the skin from the larger half without losing too much of the flesh. Cut in half lengthways, remove the seeds and cut the flesh into 5 cm/2 inch dice. Repeat with the other piece. Place on a large baking sheet, drizzle with 2 tablespoons of the olive oil and season with salt and pepper. Mix well and cook in a preheated oven, 220°C (425°F), Gas Mark 7, for 15 minutes, until soft and slightly browned.

2. Melt 50 g/2 oz of the butter with the remaining olive oil in a heavy-based saucepan. Add the garlic and onion and sauté gently for 5 minutes, until softened but not coloured.

3. Add the rice and stir well to coat the grains with oil and butter. Add the hot stock a large ladleful at a time, stirring until each addition is absorbed into the rice. Continue adding stock in this way, cooking until the rice is creamy but the grains are still firm. This should take about 20 minutes.

4. Remove the squash from the oven, add to the risotto with the Parmesan and remaining butter, season to taste with salt and pepper and stir gently. Cover the pan and leave the risotto to rest for a few minutes before serving with a little pumpkin seed oil drizzled on top of each portion.

Serves 4/ Preparation time: 10 minutes/ Cooking time: 30 minutes

Beetroot and Horseradish Risotto

This risotto makes an impressive main course for 4 people, but will also serve 6–8 as a colourful appetizer. If you can find fresh horseradish, use it in place of the bottled variety. The flavour is far superior, but beware of its heat intensity which can be anything from harmlessly mild to hot and fiery, depending on how fresh it is.

4 tablespoons olive oil

1 large red onion, chopped

3 garlic cloves, crushed

400 g/13 oz risotto rice

1.3 litres/2¼ pints hot Vegetable Stock
   (see page 19)

425 g/14 oz cooked beetroot, finely diced

4 tablespoons roughly chopped dill

1–2 tablespoons freshly grated horseradish or
   1 tablespoon hot horseradish from a jar

50 g/2 oz salted macadamia nuts or almonds

salt and pepper

mixed salad leaves, to serve

1. Heat the oil in a large, heavy-based saucepan. Add the onion and garlic and sauté gently for 5 minutes until softened but not coloured. Add the rice and stir well to coat the grains with the oil.

2. Add the hot stock, a large ladleful at a time, stirring until each addition is absorbed into the rice. Continue adding stock in this way, cooking until the rice is creamy but the grains are still firm. This should take about 20 minutes.

3. Stir in the beetroot, dill, horseradish and nuts. Season to taste with salt and pepper and heat through gently for 2–3 minutes. Cover the pan and leave the risotto to rest for a few minutes before serving with mixed salad leaves.

Serves 6/ Preparation time: 15 minutes/ Cooking time: 30 minutes

Creamy Radicchio and Pancetta Risotto

This unusual dish is from the Veneto, where rice is grown as well as several varieties of radicchio. It has both a sweet and a sharp flavour.

125 g/4 oz butter

2 carrots, finely diced

125 g/4 oz smoked pancetta, finely diced

2 garlic cloves, finely chopped

500 g/1 lb radicchio, finely shredded

500 g/1 lb risotto rice

1.5 litres/2½ pints hot Chicken or Vegetable Stock (see pages 17 and 19)

3 tablespoons single cream

75 g/3 oz Parmesan cheese, freshly grated, plus extra to serve

salt and pepper

1. Melt half of the butter in a large saucepan and add the carrots. Cook gently for 5 minutes until they start to soften. Add the pancetta and garlic and cook until just beginning to colour. Stir in the radicchio and cook until it begins to wilt.

2. Add the rice and stir well to coat the grains with the butter. Add the hot stock, a large ladleful at a time, stirring until each addition is absorbed into the rice. Continue adding stock in this way, cooking until the rice is creamy but the grains are still firm. This should take about 20 minutes. Season to taste with salt and pepper, then stir in the remaining butter, the cream and Parmesan.

3. Cover the pan and leave the risotto to rest for a few minutes before serving, sprinkled with a little grated Parmesan.

Serves 4/ Preparation time: 5–10 minutes/ Cooking time: 30 minutes

Risotto with Red Pepper and Aubergine

This colourful risotto has a robust flavour and a deliciously rich texture.

2 tablespoons olive oil

40 g/1½ oz butter

1 shallot, finely chopped

1 aubergine, finely chopped

1 red pepper, cored, deseeded and finely diced

375 g/12 oz risotto rice

50 ml/2 fl oz dry white wine

1 litre/1¾ pints hot Vegetable Stock
   (see page 19)

1 tablespoon chopped parsley

4 basil leaves, torn into small pieces (see herbs,
   page 10)

25 g/1 oz Parmesan cheese, freshly grated

2 tablespoons single cream

salt and pepper

1. Heat the oil and 25 g/1 oz of the butter in a deep pan. Add the shallot and sauté over a medium heat for 3 minutes until softened, but not coloured. Add the aubergine and diced pepper and cook over a medium high heat for about 5 minutes.

2. Add the rice and stir well to coat the grains with the butter and oil. Add the wine, bring to the boil and cook, stirring, until almost all the liquid has evaporated. Add the hot stock, a large ladleful at a time, stirring until each addition is absorbed into the rice. Continue adding stock in this way, cooking until the rice is creamy but the grains are still firm. This should take about 20 minutes.

3. Season to taste with salt and pepper, if necessary. Add the reserved butter, chopped herbs, Parmesan and cream. Mix well, cover and leave the risotto to rest for a few minutes before serving.

Asparagus and White Wine Risotto

Risotto with asparagus is a classic dish and perfect for a light lunch or supper.

1.5 litres/2½ pints Vegetable Stock (see page 19) or water

500 g/1 lb young green asparagus (whole stems), topped and tailed and peeled, with trimmings reserved

1 bay leaf

2 large onions, 1 quartered and 1 finely chopped

125 g/4 oz unsalted butter

425–500 g/14–16 oz risotto rice

300 ml/½ pint dry white wine

50 g/2 oz Parmesan cheese, thinly shaved

salt and pepper

1. Bring the stock or water to the boil in a large, heavy-based saucepan. Add the asparagus trimmings, the bay leaf and onion quarters and boil for 20 minutes. Strain into a clean pan and return the stock to the boil.
2. Meanwhile, cut the asparagus tips into 2.5–4 cm/1–1½ inch lengths. Cut half of the remaining stems into similar-size pieces and chop the rest very finely. Cook the asparagus tips and pieces of stem in the boiling stock for 3–4 minutes depending on their thickness, until just tender. Transfer the asparagus to a colander with a slotted spoon and refresh under cold running water. Drain and reserve.
3. Melt half the butter in a large, heavy-based pan over a low heat. Add the chopped onion and sauté for 5 minutes, until softened but not coloured. Add the rice and stir well to coat the grains with the butter. Add the wine, bring to the boil and cook, stirring, until almost all the liquid has evaporated.
4. Add the hot stock, a large ladleful at a time, stirring until each addition is absorbed into the rice. Continue adding stock in this way, cooking until the rice is creamy but the grains are still firm. Add all the asparagus with the final ladleful of stock. Stir in the remaining butter and season to taste with salt and pepper. Cover the pan and leave the risotto to rest for a few minutes before serving, topped with Parmesan shavings.

Serves 4/ Preparation time: 5–10 minutes/ Cooking time: 25 minutes

Asian-style Risotto

An unusual kind of risotto, this dish successfully combines the flavours of the West with Eastern ingredients.

1.2 litres/2 pints Vegetable Stock (see page 19)

1 tablespoon dark soy sauce

2 tablespoons mirin

3 tablespoons sunflower oil

1 tablespoon sesame oil

1 bunch spring onions, thickly sliced

2 garlic cloves, chopped

2.5 cm/1 inch piece of fresh root ginger, peeled and grated

375 g/12 oz risotto rice

6 lime leaves

250 g/8 oz shiitake mushrooms

15 g/½ oz coriander, chopped

coriander sprigs, to garnish

1. Put the stock, soy sauce and mirin into a pan and bring to a very gentle simmer.

2. Meanwhile, heat 2 tablespoons of the sunflower oil and the sesame oil and cook the spring onions, garlic and ginger over a high heat for 1 minute. Add the rice and lime leaves and stir well to coat the grains with the oil. Add the hot stock, a large ladleful at a time, stirring until each addition is absorbed into the rice. Continue adding stock in this way, cooking until the rice is creamy but the grains are still firm. This should take about 20 minutes.

3. Meanwhile, discard the stalks of the mushrooms and thinly slice all but a few. Fry all the mushrooms in the remaining oil for 5 minutes until golden.

4. Add the coriander to the risotto with the mushrooms. Heat through, then cover the pan and leave the risotto to rest for a few minutes before serving, garnished with the reserved whole mushrooms and coriander sprigs.

Wild Mushroom Risotto

If you are not using ceps, try to obtain two or three different of mushrooms to make a really flavourful dish. Alternatively, use a mixture of cultivated and wild mushrooms.

125 g/4 oz butter

1 large onion, finely chopped

2 garlic cloves, finely chopped

175 g/6 oz mixed wild mushrooms or ceps,
   roughly chopped

1 tablespoon chopped mixed thyme and
   marjoram

150 ml/¼ pint dry white wine

500 g/1 lb risotto rice

1.5 litres/2½ pints hot Chicken or Vegetable
   Stock (see pages 17 and 19)

salt and pepper

shredded marjoram leaves, to garnish

75 g/3 oz Parmesan cheese, freshly grated,
   to serve

1. Melt the butter in a large, heavy-based saucepan. Add the onion and garlic and sauté gently for 5 minutes, until softened, but not coloured. Stir in the mushrooms and herbs, and cook over a moderate heat for 3 minutes. Pour in the wine, bring to the boil and cook, stirring until almost all the liquid has evaporated.

2. Add the rice and stir well to coat the grains with the butter. Add the stock, a large ladleful at a time, stirring until each addition is absorbed into the rice. Continue adding the stock in this way, cooking until the rice is creamy but the grains are still firm. This should take about 20 minutes. Season to taste with salt and pepper.

3. Cover the pan and leave the risotto to rest for a few minutes, garnish with the shredded marjoram, then serve with the grated Parmesan.

Serves 6/ Preparation time: 10 minutes/ Cooking time: 30 minutes

Piedmontese Risotto

The Piedmont borders on both France and Switzerland and is a famous farming region of northern Italy. The word Piedmont literally means 'foot of the mountains'.

125 g/4 oz butter

1 large onion, finely chopped

150 ml/¼ pint dry white wine

500 g/1 lb risotto rice

pinch of saffron threads

1.5 litres/2½ pints hot Chicken or Vegetable
   Stock (see pages 17 and 19)

75 g/3 oz Parmesan cheese, freshly grated

salt and pepper

1. Melt half of the butter in a large, heavy-based saucepan. Add the onion and sauté gently for 5 minutes, until softened but not coloured. Pour in the wine, bring to the boil and cook, stirring, until almost all the liquid has evaporated.

2. Add the rice and saffron and stir well to coat the grains with the butter. Add the stock, a large ladleful at a time, and stir until each addition is absorbed into the rice. Continue adding stock in this way, cooking until the rice is creamy but the grains are still firm. This should take about 20 minutes. Season to taste with salt and pepper, then stir in the remaining butter and the Parmesan.

3. Cover the pan and leave the risotto to rest for a few minutes, then serve.

Sage and Walnut Risotto with a Cheese Crust

Try to get the freshest walnuts possible for this classic combination, as walnuts that have been stored for a long time tend to be dry and bitter.

50 g/2 oz butter

1 onion, chopped

375 g/12 oz risotto rice

1.3 litres/2¼ pints hot Vegetable Stock
   (see page 19)

2 tablespoons chopped sage

50 g/2 oz walnuts, roughly chopped

250 g/8 oz Brie cheese, thinly sliced

salt and pepper

mixed salad leaves, to serve

1. Melt the butter in a large, heavy-based saucepan. Add the onion and sauté for 5 minutes, until softened but not browned. Add the rice and stir well to coat the grains with the butter.

2. Add the hot stock, a large ladleful at a time, stirring until each addition is absorbed into the rice. Continue adding stock in this way, cooking until the rice is creamy but the grains are still firm. This should take about 20 minutes.

3. Stir in the sage and walnuts and season to taste with salt and pepper. Transfer the risotto to a shallow flameproof serving dish and cover with the slices of Brie. Cook under a preheated hot grill for about 3 minutes, until the cheese has melted. Serve with mixed salad leaves.

Serves 4/ Preparation time: 40 minutes/ Cooking time: 55–60 minutes

Onion Risotto with Sun-dried Tomatoes

25 g/1 oz butter

2 tablespoons extra virgin olive oil

500 g/1 lb baby onions

2 tablespoons chopped thyme

375 g/12 oz risotto rice

150 ml/¼ pint light red wine

900 ml/1½ pints Vegetable Stock
  (see page 19)

125 g/4 oz drained sun-dried tomatoes in oil,
  chopped

1 tablespoon balsamic vinegar

4 tablespoons crème fraîche

salt and pepper

grated Parmesan cheese, to serve

1. Melt the butter with the oil in a large frying pan, add the onions and cook over a low heat for 25 minutes until golden and caramelized, stirring occasionally.

2. Add the thyme and rice and stir well to coat the grains with the butter, oil and onions, then pour in the red wine. Boil rapidly for 5 minutes until reduced. Add the hot stock, a large ladleful at a time, stirring until each addition is absorbed into the rice. Continue adding stock in this way, cooking until the rice is creamy but the grains are still firm. This should take about 20 minutes.

3. Stir in all the remaining ingredients, season to taste with salt and pepper and serve with Parmesan.

Herby Risotto

Toma cheese from the Italian Alps is used in this aromatic risotto. If you cannot find it, use fontina or Parmesan instead.

125 g/4 oz butter

2 tablespoons olive oil

1 onion, finely chopped

1 garlic clove, finely chopped

300 g/10 oz risotto rice

1 litre/1¾ pints hot Chicken or Vegetable Stock
   (see pages 17 and 19)

handful of parsley, chopped

handful of basil, chopped

handful of oregano, chopped

handful of thyme, chopped

125 g/4 oz Toma cheese, grated

salt and pepper

herb sprigs, to garnish

1. Melt 50 g/2 oz of the butter with the olive oil in a heavy-based saucepan, add the onion and garlic and sauté for 5 minutes until softened but not coloured.

2. Add the rice and stir well to coat the grains with the butter and oil. Add the hot stock, a large ladleful at a time, stirring until each addition is absorbed into the rice. Continue adding stock in this way, cooking until the rice is creamy but the grains are still firm. This should take about 20 minutes.

3. Add the herbs, the remaining butter and the cheese and mix well. Season to taste with salt and pepper and stir well. Cover and leave the risotto to rest for a few minutes before serving, garnished with the herb sprigs.

Serves 4/ Preparation time: 10 minutes/ Cooking time: 25 minutes

Red Wine Risotto

450 ml/¾ pint Valpolicella or other red wine

600 ml/1 pint hot Chicken Stock (see page 17)

125 g/4 oz butter

1 tablespoon olive oil

2 garlic cloves, finely chopped

2 red onions, chopped

300 g/10 oz risotto rice

250 g/8 oz field mushrooms, trimmed and sliced

175 g/6 oz Parmesan cheese, freshly grated

salt and pepper

1. Heat the red wine in a large saucepan to a gentle simmer. Add the hot stock.

2. Melt 50 g/2 oz of the butter with the oil in a heavy-based saucepan. Add the garlic and onions and sauté gently for 5 minutes, until softened but not coloured.

3. Add the rice and stir well to coat the grains with the butter and oil. Add the hot stock mixture, a large ladleful at a time, stirring until each addition is absorbed into the rice. Continue adding the stock mixture in this way, cooking until the rice is creamy but the grains are still firm. This should take about 20 minutes. When half of the stock has been incorporated, add the mushrooms and season to taste with salt and pepper.

4. When all the stock has been added and the rice is just cooked, add most of the Parmesan and the remaining butter and mix well. Cover and leave the risotto to rest for a few minutes, garnish with a little grated Parmesan and serve.

Serves 4/ Preparation time: 10 minutes/ Cooking time: 20 minutes

Chestnut Risotto Cakes

These delicious little cakes are crisp on the outside yet moist and risotto-like in the centre. If you do not need the full quantity, freeze the shaped but uncooked mixture for a later date.

15 g/½ oz dried porcini mushrooms

1 tablespoon olive oil

175 g/6 oz risotto rice

600 ml/1 pint hot Vegetable Stock (see page 19)

50 g/2 oz butter

1 onion, chopped

3 garlic cloves, crushed

200 g/7 oz cooked, peeled chestnuts, chopped

75 g/3 oz Parmesan cheese, freshly grated

1 egg, lightly beaten

50 g/2 oz polenta

vegetable oil, for shallow-frying

salt and pepper

lemon wedges, to garnish

mixed salad leaves, to serve

1. Place the dried mushrooms in a bowl and cover with boiling water. Leave to stand while preparing the rice.
2. Heat the olive oil in a heavy-based saucepan. Add the rice and stir well to coat the grains with oil. Add the hot stock and bring to the boil. Reduce the heat, partially cover and simmer, stirring frequently, for 12–15 minutes, until the rice is tender and the stock is absorbed. Transfer to a bowl.
3. Meanwhile, melt the butter in a saucepan. Add the onion and garlic and sauté gently for 5 minutes. Drain and chop the mushrooms, then add them to the rice with the onion mixture, chestnuts, Parmesan and egg. Stir until well combined and season to taste with salt and pepper.
4. Divide the mixture into 12 portions. Pat each portion into a cake and roll in the polenta. Heat the oil for shallow-frying and fry the cakes for 2 minutes on each side, until golden. Garnish each serving with a lemon wedge and serve immediately with mixed salad leaves.

Fish and Shellfish

Smoked Salmon Risotto with Dill and Crème Fraîche

100 g/3½ oz smoked salmon

100 g/3½ oz mangetouts

50 g/2 oz butter

3 shallots, finely chopped

375 g/12 oz risotto rice

1.2 litres/2 pints hot Fish Stock (see page 16)

150 ml/¼ pint crème fraîche

4 tablespoons chopped dill

salt and pepper

1. Cut the salmon into small pieces. Slice the mangetouts lengthways into thin slices.

2. Melt the butter in a large, heavy-based saucepan and gently sauté the shallots for 5 minutes until softened but not coloured. Add the rice and stir well to coat the grains with the butter.

3. Add the hot stock, a large ladleful at a time, stirring until each addition is absorbed into the rice. Continue adding stock in this way, cooking until the rice is creamy but the grains are still firm. This should take about 20 minutes.

4. Add the smoked salmon, shredded mangetouts and half the crème fraîche and dill, stirring gently for about 1 minute, until the salmon has turned opaque. Season to taste with salt and pepper. Cover and leave the risotto to rest for a few minutes, then spoon over the remaining crème fraîche, if liked, and serve scattered with the remaining dill.

Serves 6–8/ Preparation time: 20 minutes/ Cooking time: 35–40 minutes

Fish Risotto

50–75 g/2–3 oz unsalted butter

1 large onion, finely chopped

1 celery stick, sliced

1 thyme sprig

2 parsley sprigs

1 mace blade

1 small onion, left whole and studded with
   2 cloves

1.2–1.5 litres/2–2½ pints hot Fish Stock
   (see page 16)

375–500 g/12 oz–1 lb risotto rice

150 ml/¼ pint dry white wine

500 g/1 lb monkfish, haddock, halibut or other
   firm white fish fillets, skinned and cubed

2 small red mullet, heads and tails removed, cut
   into 2.5 cm/1 inch slices (optional)

3–4 saffron threads (optional)

1 garlic clove, finely chopped

300 g/10 oz cooked prawns in their shells

40 g/1½ oz Parmesan cheese, freshly grated,
   plus extra to serve

sea salt and freshly ground white pepper

finely chopped parsley, to garnish

1. Heat 25 g/1 oz of the butter in a large, heavy-based pan. Add the onion and sauté for 5 minutes, until softened but not coloured.

2. Meanwhile, tie the celery, thyme, parsley, mace blade and studded onion in a piece of muslin and add to the pan of fish stock. Bring just to boiling point, then keep at a gentle simmer.

3. Add the rice (use a larger amount if omitting the mullet) to the onions and stir well to coat the grains with the butter. Pour in the wine, bring to the boil and cook, stirring, until almost all the liquid has evaporated.

4. Add the hot stock, a large ladleful at a time, stirring until each addition is absorbed into the rice. Continue adding stock in this way until you have added about 1 litre/1¾ pints.

5. Add the monkfish and red mullet slices, if using, then pour in a little more stock and cook for 4–5 minutes.

6. Put the saffron, if using, in a small bowl, pour over 3–4 tablespoons of the stock. Stir quickly to start the colour running, then set aside.

7. Melt 15 g/½ oz of the butter in a small pan, add the garlic and prawns and cook for 3–4 minutes, then stir into the risotto. Add the saffron liquid and another ladleful of stock, cooking until the rice is creamy but the grains are still firm. Season to taste with salt and pepper.

8. Add the remaining butter and the Parmesan, stirring until melted. Cover and leave the risotto to rest for a few minutes before sprinkling with parsley and serving with more Parmesan.

Seafood Risotto

In an authentic Italian risotto, such as Fish Risotto on page 56, the stock is added a ladleful at a time and fully absorbed before more is added. In this simpler version, the stock is added all at once and simmered gently until all the liquid has been absorbed.

50 g/2 oz butter

1 onion, chopped

1 yellow pepper, cored, deseeded and chopped

1 red pepper, cored, deseeded and chopped

4 tomatoes, skinned, deseeded and chopped

375 g/12 oz cod, skinned and cut into
   bite-sized pieces

8 prepared scallops

250 g/8 oz risotto rice

475 ml/16 fl oz hot Fish Stock (see page 16)

salt and pepper

1 tablespoon finely chopped parsley, to garnish

2 tablespoons freshly grated Parmesan cheese,
   to serve

1. Melt half of the butter in a heavy-based saucepan. Add the onion, yellow and red peppers and tomatoes and sauté gently for 2 minutes until softened but not coloured.

2. Add the cod and scallops, and cook for a further 3 minutes. Transfer to a bowl and season with salt and pepper. Cover and set aside.

3. Melt the remaining butter in the pan, add the rice and stir well to coat the grains with the butter. Stir in the stock and 1 teaspoon of salt. Bring to the boil, lower the heat and cover the pan. Simmer for 15 minutes, until the rice is almost tender and the liquid has been absorbed.

4. Gently stir in the cod mixture and heat for 2 minutes. Garnish the risotto with parsley, sprinkle with Parmesan cheese and serve immediately.

Serves 6/ Preparation time: 25 minutes/ Cooking Time: 1 hour

Saffron Seafood Risotto

2 large pinches of saffron threads

375 g/12 oz raw prawns in their shells

1.5 litres/2½ pints hot Fish Stock (see page 16)

300 ml/½ pint dry white wine

6 baby squid, cleaned

6 scallops

500 g/1 lb mussels

250 g/8 oz small clams

75 g/3 oz butter

1 onion, finely chopped

500 g/1 lb risotto rice

3 tablespoons chopped parsley, to garnish

1. Put the saffron threads in a small bowl, cover with warm water, stir and set aside to soak.
2. Remove the heads from the prawns and put the heads into a large saucepan with the stock and wine. Bring to the boil, cover the pan and simmer for 20 minutes.
3. Cut the squid into rings and trim the tentacles. Remove the hard white muscle from the side of each scallop and separate the white flesh from the orange corals. Scrub the mussels well and pull off any beards. Discard any with damaged shells or that do not close when sharply tapped. Rinse the clams well.
4. Strain the prawn stock into a clean saucepan and bring to simmering point. Add the prawns and cook for 2 minutes. Add the squid, scallops and their corals and cook for a further 2 minutes. Remove all the seafood with a slotted spoon and set aside. Put the mussels and clams into the stock and bring to the boil. Cover and cook for 5 minutes, or until all the shellfish have opened. Remove with a slotted spoon. Discard any that remain closed.
5. Melt the butter in a large saucepan. Add the onion and sauté for 5 minutes, until softened but not coloured. Add the rice and stir well to coat the grains with the butter. Add the hot stock, a large ladleful at a time, stirring until each addition is absorbed into the rice. Continue adding stock in this way, cooking until only 2 ladlefuls of stock remain and the rice is creamy but the grains are still firm. This should take about 20 minutes. Season to taste with salt and pepper.
6. Finally, stir in the remaining stock, the infused saffron liquid and all the seafood, cover and cook gently for 5 minutes, or until piping hot. Leave the risotto to rest for a few minutes before serving, sprinkled with the parsley.

Roast Cod and Olive Risotto

This dish would work equally well with most firm-fleshed white fish, such as monkfish or haddock.

500 g/1 lb cod fillet, skinned

600 ml/1 pint white wine

600 ml/1 pint hot Fish Stock (see page 16)

50 g/2 oz butter

2 onions, chopped

375 g/12 oz risotto rice

50 g/2 oz sun-dried tomatoes in oil, drained and
    sliced

4 tablespoons olive oil

2 tablespoons chopped oregano

200 g/7 oz cherry tomatoes, halved

50 g/2 oz Parmesan cheese, grated

50 g/2 oz pitted black olives, chopped

1 tablespoon white wine vinegar

salt and pepper

1. Pat the fish dry on kitchen paper and cut into 4 pieces. Season with salt and pepper. Put the wine and stock in a saucepan and bring almost to the boil. Melt the butter in a large, heavy-based saucepan and sauté the onions for 5 minutes, until softened but not coloured.

2. Add the rice and sun-dried tomatoes and stir well to coat the grains with the butter. Add the hot stock mixture, a large ladleful at a time, stirring until each addition is absorbed into the rice. Continue adding stock in this way, cooking until the rice is creamy but the grains are still firm. This should take about 20 minutes.

3. Meanwhile, heat 2 tablespoons of the oil in a large frying pan and cook the fish for 3 minutes on each side, until cooked through. Drain and keep warm. Add the oregano and cherry tomatoes to the pan and cook for 1 minute. Season lightly with salt and pepper.

4. Stir the cheese into the risotto and pile on to serving plates. Top with the fish and cherry tomatoes. Add the olives, the remaining oil and the vinegar to the frying pan, stirring for a few seconds, then pour over the fish to serve.

Serves 4–6/ Preparation time: 15 minutes/ Cooking time: 40 minutes

Smoked Haddock Risotto

Try to find undyed smoked haddock, as it has a much better flavour and is far healthier than the bright
yellow chemically treated fish.

500 g/1 lb smoked haddock fillet, skinned

1.2 litres/2 pints water

2–3 saffron threads

25 g/1 oz butter

4 shallots, finely chopped

2 garlic cloves, crushed

1 tablespoon chopped sage

375 g/12 oz risotto rice

150 ml/¼ pint dry white wine

4 tablespoons crème fraîche or double cream

25 g/1 oz Parmesan cheese, freshly grated

2 tablespoons olive oil

12 large sage leaves

salt and pepper

1. Pull out and discard any bones that may remain in the haddock. Place the fish in a large frying pan and pour in the water. Bring to the boil over a low heat and simmer gently for 5 minutes. Lift out the fish, flake into large pieces and set aside. Strain the cooking liquid into a saucepan and add the saffron threads. Leave to infuse for 10 minutes

2. Melt the butter in a large nonstick frying pan. Add the shallots, garlic and sage and sauté for 5 minutes, until softened but not brown. Add the rice and stir well to coat the grains with the butter. Pour in the wine, bring to the boil and cook, stirring, until almost all the liquid has evaporated.

3. Meanwhile, bring the saffron stock to a gentle simmer. Add the hot stock, a large ladleful at a time, stirring until each addition is absorbed into the rice. Continue adding stock in this way, cooking until the rice is creamy but the grains are still firm. This will take about 20 minutes.

4. Stir in the crème fraîche or double cream, Parmesan and season to taste with salt and pepper and arrange the flaked fish on top. Cover loosely with foil. Heat the oil in a small frying pan and fry the sage leaves for 1 minute, until crispy. Serve the risotto garnished with the sage leaves.

Tuna and Fennel Risotto

Virtually a storecupboard recipe, this risotto-style dish is a good choice for a midweek family supper.

1 tablespoon vegetable oil

1 onion, chopped

2 rindless streaky bacon rashers, chopped

1 fennel bulb, chopped

125 g/4 oz button mushrooms, sliced

250 g/8 oz long-grain rice

400 g/13 oz can chopped tomatoes

2 teaspoons tomato purée

300 ml/½ pint hot Vegetable Stock (see page 19)
   or water

grated rind of 1 lemon

1 tablespoon lemon juice

dash of Tabasco sauce

200 g/7 oz can tuna in oil, drained

50 g/2 oz frozen peas

1 tablespoon freshly grated Parmesan cheese

fresh fennel fronds and slices, to garnish

salt and pepper

1. Heat the oil in a medium saucepan. Add the onion, bacon and fennel and cook for 5 minutes, until tender.

2. Add the mushrooms and rice and stir well to coat the grains with the oil. Add the tomatoes, tomato purée, stock, lemon rind and juice and season to taste with Tabasco sauce, salt and pepper.

3. Bring to the boil, stirring, then reduce the heat, cover and cook gently for 5 minutes.

4. Flake the tuna with a fork and add it to the rice mixture with the peas. Continue cooking for 5–8 minutes, until most of the liquid has been absorbed and the rice grains are tender.

5. Place the risotto in a warmed serving dish, sprinkle with Parmesan and garnish with fennel fronds and slices.

Serves 4/ Preparation time: 10 minutes/ Cooking time: 40 minutes

Roasted Monkfish and Pepper Risotto

Roast vegetables, especially peppers, have a delicious sweet flavour that goes well with meaty monkfish and rice.

3 red peppers, cored, deseeded and cut into
   large chunks

2 small red onions, cut into thin wedges

4 tablespoons olive oil

4 garlic cloves, crushed

2 tablespoons chopped oregano

500 g/1 lb monkfish

50 g/2 oz butter

375 g/12 oz risotto rice

150 ml/¼ pint dry white wine

1.3 litres/2¼ pints hot Fish Stock (see page 16)

4 tablespoons dry vermouth, (optional)

salt and pepper

oregano sprig, to garnish

1. Scatter the peppers and onion wedges in a large roasting tin. Mix the oil with the garlic and oregano, season with salt and pepper and toss with the peppers and onions. Roast in a preheated oven, 220°C (425°F), Gas Mark 7 for 20 minutes, until beginning to brown.

2. Meanwhile, cut the monkfish fillets away from the central bone and pat dry on kitchen paper. Slice into small chunks and add to the roasting tin, tossing the ingredients together. Return to the oven for a further 15–20 minutes, until the vegetables are roasted and the fish is cooked through.

3. While the fish is roasting, melt the butter in a large, heavy-based frying pan. Add the rice and stir well to coat the grains with the butter. Add the wine, bring to the boil and cook, stirring, until almost all the liquid has evaporated. Add the hot stock, a large ladleful at a time, stirring until each addition is absorbed into the rice. Continue adding stock in this way, cooking until the rice is creamy but the grains are still firm. This should take about 20 minutes.

4. Stir the roasted ingredients, any roasting juices and the vermouth, if using, into the risotto. Season to taste with salt and pepper and serve garnished with an oregano sprig.

Red Snapper and Bacon Risotto

Snapper has delicate yet firm flesh with a truly wonderful flavour. If you are buying whole snapper or they are being filleted for you, make sure you keep the heads and bones, as they are rich in gelatine and make excellent stock.

4 large or 8 small red snapper fillets

50 g/2 oz butter

1 tablespoon olive oil

150 g/5 oz smoked streaky bacon, thinly sliced

2 small leeks, chopped

375 g/12 oz risotto rice

2 garlic cloves, crushed

1.3 litres/2¼ pints hot Fish Stock (see page 16)

3 tablespoons chopped fennel

salt and pepper

red chilli slices, to garnish (optional)

1. Pat the fish dry on kitchen paper and season lightly with salt and pepper. Melt 15 g/½ oz of the butter in a frying pan with the oil and fry the fish fillets for 1–2 minutes on each side, until cooked through. Remove from the pan and set aside.

2. Melt the remaining butter in a large, heavy-based saucepan. Add the bacon and cook for 3–4 minutes, until browned. Remove with a slotted spoon. Add the leeks to the pan and cook gently for 2 minutes. Add the rice to the pan and stir well to coat the grains with the butter.

3. Return the bacon to the pan and add the garlic. Add the hot stock, a large ladleful at a time, stirring until each addition is absorbed into the rice. Continue adding stock in this way, cooking until the rice is creamy but the grains are still firm. This should take about 20 minutes.

4. Add the fennel and a little pepper and gently fold in the fish fillets. Heat for 1 minute before serving. Serve garnished with some red chilli slices, if liked.

Serves 4/ Preparation time: 10 minutes/ Cooking time: 30 minutes

Thai-style Crab Risotto

This risotto tastes best when made with fresh crab meat, but you could use thawed, frozen crab meat if necessary.

75 g/3 oz creamed coconut

1 lemon grass stalk

3 tablespoons sunflower oil

1 bunch of spring onions, sliced

3 garlic cloves, sliced

2.5 cm/1 inch piece of fresh root ginger, peeled and chopped

375 g/12 oz risotto rice

1.3 litres/2¼ pints hot Fish Stock (see page 16)

2 tablespoons lime juice

1 small fresh dressed crab

salt and pepper

chopped coriander leaves, to serve

red chilli slices, to garnish

1. Chop the creamed coconut into small pieces. Bruise the lemon grass with a rolling pin and slice as thinly as possible.

2. Heat the oil in a large, heavy-based saucepan. Add the spring onions, lemon grass, garlic and ginger and sauté for 3 minutes. Add the rice and stir well to coat the grains with the oil.

3. Add the hot stock, a large ladleful at a time, stirring until each addition is absorbed into the rice. Continue adding stock in this way, cooking until the rice is creamy but the grains are still firm. This should take about 20 minutes. Add the creamed coconut with the last of the stock.

4. Add the lime juice and crab, stirring to break it up and heat through. Cover and leave the risotto to rest for a few minutes before serving, scattered with plenty of coriander and garnished with chilli slices.

Squid Risotto

The key to success with squid is to cook it quickly, otherwise it becomes rubbery and inedible.

500 g/1 lb prepared squid tubes

50 g/2 oz butter

2 garlic cloves, crushed

1 onion, chopped

400 g/13 oz risotto rice

1.3 litres/2¼ pints hot Fish Stock (see page 16)

15 g/½ oz flat leaf parsley, chopped

3 tablespoons capers, rinsed

finely grated rind of 2 lemons

salt and pepper

1. Slice the squid into rings and pat dry on kitchen paper. Melt the butter in a large heavy-based saucepan. Add the squid and garlic and sauté gently for 3–4 minutes, until the squid puffs up. Remove from the pan with a slotted spoon.

2. Add the onion to the pan and sauté gently for 5 minutes, until softened but not coloured. Add the hot stock, a large ladleful at a time, stirring until each addition is absorbed into the rice. Continue adding stock in this way, cooking until the rice is creamy but the grains are still firm. This should take about 20 minutes.

3. Return the squid and any cooking juices to the pan with the parsley, capers and lemon rind and season to taste with salt and pepper. Heat through for 1 minute, cover and leave the risotto to rest for a few minutes before serving.

Anchovy and Tomato Risotto

If you find anchovies too salty, soak them in a little milk, then pat dry before using. In any case, be careful when you add seasoning, as extra salt may not be required.

50 g/2 oz butter

1 onion, chopped

1 small leek, diced

400 g/13 oz risotto rice

3 tablespoons sun-dried tomato paste

1.3 litres/2¼ pints hot Fish Stock (see page 16)

50 g/2 oz can anchovies, drained and chopped

500 g/1 lb tomatoes, deseeded and sliced

small handful flat leaf parsley, chopped

salt and pepper

flat leaf parsley sprigs, to garnish

1. Melt the butter in a large, heavy-based saucepan. Add the onion and leek and sauté for 5 minutes, until softened. Add the rice and stir well to coat the grains with the butter. Stir in the tomato paste.

2. Add the hot stock, a large ladleful at a time, stirring until each addition is absorbed into the rice. Continue adding stock in this way, cooking until the rice is creamy but the grains are still firm. This should take about 20 minutes.

3. Add the anchovies to the pan with the tomato pieces and parsley and season to taste with salt and pepper, if required. Heat through for 1 minute, cover and leave the risotto to rest for a few minutes before serving garnished with parsley sprigs.

Serves 4/ Preparation time: 10 minutes/ Cooking time: 30 minutes

Mussel Risotto

1 kg/2 lb fresh mussels

50 g/2 oz butter

1 fennel bulb, chopped

150 ml/¼ pint dry white wine

2 garlic cloves, crushed

375 g/12 oz risotto rice

6 large thyme sprigs

1 teaspoon medium curry paste

1.2 litres/2 pints hot Fish Stock (see page 16)

3 tablespoons double cream

salt and pepper

chopped parsley, to garnish

1. Scrub the mussels, discarding any with damaged shells or that do not close when sharply tapped. Melt 25 g/1 oz of the butter in a large saucepan. Add the fennel and sauté for 3 minutes. Add the wine and bring to the boil.

2. Tip the mussels into the pan and cover tightly. Cook over a high heat, shaking the pan occasionally, for about 5 minutes, until the shells have opened. Drain the mussels, reserving the cooking juices. Shell about half the mussels.

3. Melt the remaining butter in a large heavy-based saucepan. Add the garlic, rice, thyme and curry paste and cook for 1 minute, stirring. Add the reserved cooking juices and cook, stirring, until the juices have been absorbed by the rice.

4. Add the hot stock, a large ladleful at a time, stirring until each addition is absorbed into the rice. Continue adding stock in this way, cooking until the rice is creamy but the grains are still firm. This should take about 20 minutes. Stir in the cream and all the mussels and cook for 1 minute. Season to taste with salt and pepper, cover and leave the risotto to rest for a few minutes before serving, sprinkled with parsley.

Serves 4–6/ Preparation time: 10 minutes/ Cooking time: 35 minutes

Prawn, Asparagus and Olive Risotto

A luxurious risotto with some unusual and subtle flavours, this makes a good dinner party dish. Olive paste is available from Italian delicatessens and many supermarkets, alternatively you can make your own (see page 13).

600 ml/1 pint water

500 g/1 lb asparagus spears, cut into
  5 cm/2 inch lengths

6 tablespoons olive oil

4 shallots, chopped

2 garlic cloves, crushed

2 teaspoons chopped thyme

375 g/12 oz risotto rice

150 ml/¼ pint dry white wine

600 ml/1 pint hot Vegetable Stock (see page 19)

500 g/1 lb small raw prawns, peeled

50 g/2 oz olive paste (pasta di olive)

3 tablespoons torn basil leaves

Parmesan cheese shavings, to serve

1. Bring the water to the boil in a large saucepan. Add the asparagus and cook for 3 minutes. Strain, reserving the liquid, and immediately refresh the asparagus under cold water. Drain well and set aside.

2. Heat the oil in a large frying pan. Add the shallots, garlic and thyme and sauté for 5 minutes. Add the rice and stir well to coat the grains with the oil. Pour in the wine, bring to the boil and cook, stirring, until almost all the liquid has evaporated.

3. Meanwhile, put the reserved asparagus liquid and vegetable stock into a small saucepan and bring to a very low simmer. Add the hot stock to the frying pan, a large ladleful at a time, stirring until each addition is absorbed into the rice. Continue adding stock in this way, cooking until the rice is creamy but the grains are still firm. This should take about 20 minutes.

4. Add the prawns and the asparagus to the rice with the final addition of stock and stir for a further 5 minutes, until the prawns and rice are cooked. Stir in the olive paste and basil and season to taste with salt and pepper. Cover and leave the risotto to rest for a few minutes before serving with plenty of Parmesan shavings.

Serves 4–6/ Preparation time: 10–15 minutes/ Cooking time: 1 hour

Prawn and Fennel Risotto

The sweet, aniseed flavour of fennel gives this risotto a delicious piquancy.

500 g/1 lb raw prawns in their shells

1 small fennel bulb, sliced

4 parsley sprigs

½ onion, roughly chopped

1 small carrot, roughly chopped

1 litre/1¾ pints water

300 ml/½ pint dry white wine

125 g/4 oz butter

2 tablespoons olive oil

500 g/1 lb risotto rice

1 garlic clove, crushed

grated rind of ½ lemon

fennel fronds, chopped

50 g/2 oz Parmesan cheese, freshly grated

salt and pepper

1. Peel the prawns and reserve the shells and heads. Put the shells, heads and any roe into a large saucepan. Add the fennel, parsley, onion, carrot and water. Bring to the boil, then simmer gently for 25–30 minutes.

2. Strain the stock, measure and make up to 1.6 litres/2¾ pints with the white wine and extra water if necessary. Bring to the boil in a clean pan and simmer gently.

3. Melt half the butter with the oil in a large heavy-based saucepan. Add the rice and stir well to coat the grains with the butter and oil. Add the hot stock, a large ladleful at a time, stirring until each addition is absorbed into the rice. Continue adding stock in this way, cooking until the rice is creamy but the grains are still firm. This should take about 20 minutes. Season to taste with salt and pepper.

4. Melt the remaining butter in a small pan, and stir in the prawns, garlic, lemon rind and fennel fronds. Stir into the rice with the Parmesan. Cover and leave the risotto to rest for a few minutes before serving.

Pea and Prawn Risotto

500 g/1 lb raw prawns

125 g/4 oz butter

1 onion, finely chopped

2 garlic cloves, crushed

250 g/8 oz risotto rice

375 g/12 oz shelled peas

150 ml/¼ pint dry white wine

1.5 litres/2½ pints hot Vegetable Stock (see page 19)

4 tablespoons chopped mint

salt and pepper

1. Peel the prawns, reserving the heads and shells.
2. Melt half of the butter in a large frying pan. Add the prawn heads and shells and stir-fry for 3–4 minutes. Strain the butter and return it to the pan.
3. Add a further 25 g/1 oz of the butter to the pan. Add the onion and garlic and sauté for 5 minutes, until softened but not coloured. Add the rice and stir well to coat the grains with the butter. Add the peas, then pour in the wine. Bring to the boil and cook, stirring, until reduced by half.
4. Add the hot stock, a large ladleful at a time, stirring until each addition is absorbed into the rice. Continue adding stock in this way, cooking until the rice is creamy, but the grains are still firm. This should take about 20 minutes.
5. Melt the remaining butter and stir-fry the prawns for 3–4 minutes, then stir them into the rice with the pan juices and mint and season to taste with salt and pepper. Cover the pan and leave the risotto to rest for a few minutes before serving.

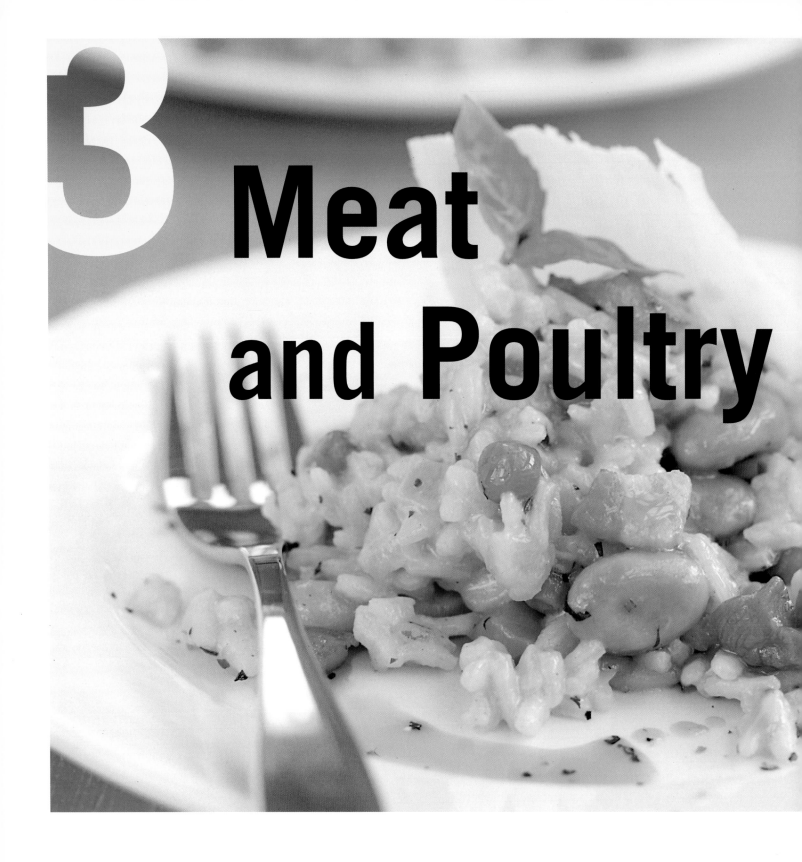

3 Meat and Poultry

Serves 4/ Preparation time: 10 minutes/ Cooking time: 30 minutes

Chorizo and Sun-dried Tomato Risotto

50 g/2 oz butter

1 tablespoon olive oil

150 g/5 oz chorizo sausage, thinly sliced

100 g/3½ oz pine nuts

1 red onion, finely chopped

1 small red chilli, cored, deseeded and thinly
   sliced

2 bay leaves

400 g/13 oz risotto rice

1.3 litres/2¼ pints hot Chicken Stock
   (see page 17)

75 g/3 oz sun-dried tomatoes in oil, drained and
   thinly sliced

small handful of coriander leaves, roughly
   chopped

salt and pepper

mixed leaf salad, to serve (optional)

1. Melt the butter with the oil in a large, heavy-based saucepan. Add the chorizo and pine nuts and fry for 2 minutes, or until the sausage begins to colour. Remove the chorizo and nuts with a slotted spoon.
2. Add the onion, chilli and bay leaves to the pan and sauté for 2 minutes. Add the rice and stir well to coat the grains with the butter and oil.
3. Add the hot stock, a large ladleful at a time, stirring until each addition is absorbed into the rice. Continue adding stock in this way, cooking until the rice is creamy but the grains are still firm. This should take about 20 minutes.
4. Return the chorizo and pine nuts to the pan and stir in the sun-dried tomatoes and coriander leaves. Cook for 1 minute. Cover and leave the risotto to rest for a few minutes before serving with a mixed leaf salad, if liked.

Sage and Lentil Risotto with Herb Sausages

100 g/3½ oz Puy lentils

8 herb sausages

50 g/2 oz butter

2 onions, sliced

375 g/12 oz risotto rice

1.2 litres/ 2 pints hot Chicken Stock
(see page 17)

8 large sage leaves, finely shredded, plus extra
to garnish (optional)

salt and pepper

1. Rinse the lentils, put them in a saucepan and cover with water. Bring to the boil and simmer for about 25 minutes, until tender. While the lentils are simmering, cook the sausages in a preheated oven, 200°C (400°F), Gas Mark 6, for 20 minutes, or until golden.

2. Meanwhile, melt the butter in a large heavy-based saucepan. Add the onions and sauté for 5 minutes, until softened but not coloured. Add the rice and stir well to coat the grains with the butter.

3. Add the shredded sage leaves to the rice. Add the hot stock, a large ladleful at a time, stirring until each addition is absorbed into the rice. Continue adding stock in this way, cooking until the rice is creamy but the grains are still firm. This should take about 20 minutes.

4. Drain the lentils and add to the pan. Season to taste with salt and pepper, cover and leave the risotto to rest for a few minutes before serving. Top with the sausages and serve garnished with sage leaves, if liked.

Roasted Pork, Parsnip and Apple Risotto

This would make a delicious change from a traditional Sunday roast.

425 g/14 oz boneless, lean belly pork or
   pancetta

425 g/14 oz slender parsnips

2 tablespoons sunflower oil

2 tart dessert apples, peeled, cored and
   thickly sliced

50 g/2 oz butter

1 onion, chopped

375 g/12 oz risotto rice

6 large sage leaves, shredded

150 ml/¼ pint dry white wine

1.2 litres/2 pints hot Chicken Stock
   (see page 17)

salt and pepper

1. Thinly slice the belly pork or roughly chop the pancetta. Quarter the parsnips lengthways and toss with the meat and oil in a large roasting tin. Bake in a preheated oven, 220°C (425°F), Gas Mark 7, for 25 minutes, until beginning to colour. Add the apple slices, stir to combine and roast for a further 20–25 minutes until golden.

2. Meanwhile, melt the butter in a large, heavy-based saucepan. Add the onion and sauté gently for 5 minutes, until softened but not coloured. Add the rice and sage and stir well to coat the grains with the butter. Add the wine, bring to the boil and cook, stirring, until almost all the liquid has evaporated.

3. Add the hot stock, a large ladleful at a time, stirring until each addition is absorbed into the rice. Continue adding stock in this way, cooking until the rice is creamy but the grains are still firm. This should take about 20 minutes.

4. Tip the ingredients from the roasting tin into the risotto, season to taste with salt and pepper and stir together for 1 minute. Cover and leave the risotto to rest for a few minutes before serving.

Pepperoni and Wilted Spinach Risotto

50 g/2 oz butter

1 tablespoon olive oil

100 g/3½ oz pepperoni sausage, thinly sliced

75 g/3 oz pine nuts

1 tablespoon paprika

2 garlic cloves, crushed

375 g/12 oz risotto rice

1.2 litres/ 2 pints hot Chicken Stock
   (see page 17)

250 g/8 oz baby spinach leaves

75 g/3 oz raisins

salt and pepper

1. Melt the butter with the oil in a large, heavy-based saucepan. Add the sausage and pine nuts and cook gently for about 3 minutes, or until the pine nuts are golden. Drain with a slotted spoon.

2. Add the paprika, garlic and rice to the pan and stir well to coat the grains with the butter and oil. Add the hot stock, a large ladleful at a time, stirring until each addition is absorbed into the rice. Continue adding stock in this way, cooking until the rice is creamy but the grains are still firm. This should take about 20 minutes.

3. Return the sliced sausage and pine nuts to the pan with the spinach and raisins. Cook over a gentle heat, stirring the spinach into the rice until wilted. Season to taste with salt and pepper. Cover and leave the risotto to rest for a few minutes before serving.

Serves 4/ Preparation time: 10 minutes/ Cooking time 35 minutes

Gingered Beef and Walnut Risotto

425 g/14 oz fillet steak

50 g/2 oz butter

100 g/3½ oz walnut pieces

1 bunch of spring onions, chopped

2 garlic cloves, chopped

375 g/12 oz risotto rice

1.3 litres/2¼ pints hot Chicken or Vegetable
    Stock (see pages 17 and 19)

50 g/2 oz piece of fresh root ginger, peeled
    and grated

2 tablespoons sunflower oil

1 tablespoon soy sauce

200 g/7 oz pak choi, roughly sliced

2 tablespoons water

salt and pepper

1. Pat the beef dry on kitchen paper and season with salt and pepper.
2. Melt the butter in a large, heavy-based saucepan. Add the walnuts and cook, stirring until beginning to brown. Remove with a slotted spoon. Add the spring onions and cook for 1 minute.
3. Add the garlic and rice to the pan and stir well to coat the grains with the butter. Add the hot stock, a large ladleful at a time, stirring until each addition is absorbed into the rice. Continue adding stock in this way, cooking until the rice is creamy but the grains are still firm. This should take about 20 minutes. Add the grated ginger with the last of the stock.
4. Meanwhile, heat the oil in a frying pan and gently cook the beef, turning frequently, for 10 minutes, until well browned. Remove from the heat and spoon the soy sauce over the beef.
5. Stir the pak choi into the risotto and season to taste with salt and pepper. Cover the risotto and leave to rest for a few minutes. Meanwhile, drain the beef and slice as thinly as possible. Pile the risotto on to serving plates and serve with the beef and walnuts. Stir the water into the frying pan, scraping up any sediment from the bottom. Spoon over the beef and serve.

Serves 4/ Preparation time: 10 minutes/ Cooking time: 25 minutes

Parma Ham and Sweet Potato Risotto

Although Parma ham and other types of prosciutto are expensive, their flavour is unique and irreplaceable.

2 medium sweet potatoes, scrubbed

50 g/2 oz butter

1 bunch of spring onions, finely sliced

375 g/12 oz risotto rice

2 bay leaves

1.2 litres/2 pints hot Chicken or Vegetable Stock
   (see pages 17 and 19)

3 tablespoons olive oil

75 g/3 oz Parma ham, torn into pieces

25 g/1 oz chopped mixed herbs, such as parsley,
   chervil, tarragon, and chives

salt and pepper

1. Cut the potatoes into 1 cm/½ inch chunks and cook in lightly salted, boiling water for 2–3 minutes to soften. Drain and reserve.

2. Melt the butter in a large, heavy-based saucepan. Add the spring onions and sauté for 1 minute. Add the rice and stir well to coat the grains with the butter.

3. Add the bay leaves to the rice. Add the hot stock, a large ladleful at a time, stirring until each addition is absorbed into the rice. Continue adding stock in this way, cooking until the rice is creamy but the grains are still firm. This should take about 20 minutes.

4. Meanwhile, heat 1 tablespoon of the oil in a frying pan and cook the ham until golden. Drain and keep warm. Add the remaining oil and fry the sweet potatoes, turning frequently, for 6–8 minutes, until golden.

5. Add the herbs to the risotto and season to taste with salt and pepper, then add the ham and sweet potatoes, folding in gently. Cover and leave the risotto to rest for a few minutes before serving.

Serves 4/ Preparation time: 10 minutes/ Cooking time: 20 minutes

Risotto alla Milanese

Virtually every town and city in northern Italy has its own speciality risotto. This
version from Milan is always served with osso buco.

75 g/3 oz butter

1 tablespoon olive oil

2 onions, finely diced

425 g/14 oz risotto rice

1 litre/1¾ pints hot Chicken Stock (see page 17)

½ teaspoon saffron threads

125 ml/4 fl oz dry vermouth or dry white wine

125 g/4 oz Parmesan cheese, freshly grated

salt and pepper

1. Melt 50 g/2 oz of the butter with the olive oil in a large heavy-based saucepan.
   Add the onions and sauté for 5 minutes until softened but not coloured.
2. Add the rice to the onions and stir well to coat the grains with the butter.
3. Add the hot stock, a large ladleful at a time, stirring until each addition is
   absorbed into the rice. Continue adding stock in this way until you have added
   about half, then add the saffron and stir well. Continue adding the stock, cooking
   until the rice is creamy but the grains are still firm. This should take about
   20 minutes in all.
4. Finally add the vermouth or white wine, Parmesan and the remaining butter in
   small knobs. Season to taste with salt and pepper. Stir well, cover and leave the
   risotto to rest for a few minutes before serving.

Serves 4–6/ Preparation time: 15 minutes/ Cooking time: about 1 hour

Risotto alla Fiorentina

2 tablespoons olive oil

65 g/2½ oz butter, softened

1 onion, sliced

250 g/8 oz minced beef

125 g/4 oz lambs' kidneys, sliced

1 chicken liver, sliced

400 g/13 oz tomatoes, skinned and mashed

400 g/13 oz risotto rice

1 litre/1¾ pints hot Beef Stock (see page 18)

75 g/3 oz Parmesan cheese, freshly grated

salt and pepper

1. Heat the oil and half the butter in a heavy-based saucepan. Add the onion and sauté gently for 5 minutes, until softened but not coloured. Add the minced beef, kidneys and chicken liver, increase the heat and cook, stirring, until browned. Add the tomatoes and season to taste with salt and pepper, lower the heat and cook for 30 minutes.

2. Add the rice and stir well to coat the grains with the butter and oil. Add the hot stock, a large ladleful at a time, stirring until each addition is absorbed into the rice. Continue adding stock in this way, cooking until the rice is creamy but the grains are still firm. This should take about 20 minutes.

3. Remove the pan from the heat. Stir in the remaining butter and the Parmesan and fold gently to mix. Cover and leave the risotto to rest for a few minutes before serving.

Serves 4/ Preparation time: 15 minutes/ Cooking time: 35 minutes

Chestnut, Bacon and Thyme Risotto

Chestnuts play an important role in the traditional cooking of both Tuscany and Liguria.

3 tablespoons olive oil

1 onion, finely chopped

3 garlic cloves, finely chopped

4 bacon rashers or prosciutto slices, diced

125 g/4 oz cooked, peeled chestnuts,
    roughly chopped

400 g/13 oz risotto rice

2 tablespoons chopped thyme

125 ml/4 fl oz dry sherry or white wine

1.2 litres/2 pints hot Vegetable Stock
    (see page 19)

50 g/2 oz Parmesan cheese, freshly grated, plus
    extra to garnish

salt and pepper

knob of butter, to garnish (optional)

green salad, to serve (optional)

1. Heat the oil in a frying pan. Add the onion and garlic and sauté for 5 minutes, until softened but not coloured. Add the bacon or prosciutto and cook for a further 5–6 minutes, until the bacon is crisp and just starting to brown.

2. Add the chestnuts and the rice to the frying pan and stir well to coat the grains with the oil. Stir in the thyme and sherry.

3. Add the hot stock, a large ladleful at a time, stirring until each addition is absorbed into the rice. Continue adding stock in this way, cooking until the rice is creamy but the grains are still firm. This should take about 20 minutes.

4. Stir the grated Parmesan into the risotto and season to taste with salt and pepper. Cover and leave to rest for a few minutes before serving, garnished with extra Parmesan, plus a knob of butter, if you like. Serve with a green salad, if liked.

Serves 2/ Preparation time: 10 minutes/ Cooking time: 35 minutes

Broad Bean, Pancetta and Fontina Risotto

An everyday Italian cheese, fontina is used here with Parmesan to give a good flavour to this broad bean risotto.

3 tablespoons olive oil

1 onion, finely chopped

3 garlic cloves, crushed

75 g/3 oz pancetta, chopped

250 g/8 oz risotto rice

½ teaspoon dried mixed herbs

900 ml/1½ pints hot Chicken or Vegetable Stock
  (see pages 17 and 19)

125 g/4 oz broad beans, thawed if frozen

75 g/3 oz peas

75 g/3 oz fontina cheese, coarsely grated

50 g/2 oz butter

2 tablespoons freshly grated Parmesan cheese,
  plus extra shavings to serve

1 tablespoon chopped mint leaves

6–8 basil leaves, torn, plus extra to serve

salt and pepper

1. Heat the olive oil in a large saucepan. Add the onion and sauté for 5 minutes, until softened but not coloured. Add the crushed garlic and pancetta to the pan and cook until the pancetta is golden brown. Add the rice and stir well to coat the grains with the oil.

2. With the pan still over a medium heat, add the dried mixed herbs and the hot stock to the rice and bring the mixture to the boil, stirring constantly. Season to taste with salt and pepper. Reduce to a simmer and simmer for 10 minutes, stirring frequently. Add the broad beans and peas to the pan and continue to cook for a further 10 minutes.

3. Remove the pan from the heat and stir in the grated fontina. Dot the butter on top with the grated Parmesan. Cover and leave the risotto to rest for a few minutes.

4. Remove the lid and add the chopped mint and torn and gently stir the cheese, butter and herbs through the risotto. Serve immediately with basil leaves and extra shavings of Parmesan.

Serves 4/ Preparation time: 10 minutes/Cooking time: about 30 minutes

Spiced Lamb Risotto with Apricots

Lamb is quite a rich meat, so it superbly complemented by the subtle sharpness of the dried fruit in this Moroccan-inspired risotto.

425 g/14 oz lean lamb fillet or boneless leg

50 g/2 oz butter

40 g/1½ oz flaked almonds

2 small onions, chopped

1 celery stick, sliced

1 cinnamon stick, halved

good pinch of saffron threads (optional)

2.5 cm/1 inch piece of fresh root ginger, peeled
  and grated

2 garlic cloves, crushed

400 g/13 oz risotto rice

1.3 litres/2¼ pints hot Chicken Stock
  (see page 17)

75 g/3 oz ready-to-eat dried apricots,
  thinly sliced

small handful of coriander, chopped

salt and pepper

1. Cut the lamb into small dice, trimming off and discarding any fat. Pat dry on kitchen paper and season with salt and pepper.
2. Melt the butter in a large, heavy-based saucepan. Add the lamb and cook, stirring, for 5 minutes until browned. Remove with a slotted spoon. Add the almonds to the pan and cook gently until golden. Remove and set aside.
3. Add the onions and celery to the pan and sauté gently for 5 minutes. Stir in the cinnamon, saffron, ginger, garlic and rice and stir well to coat the grains with the butter. Add the hot stock, a large ladleful at a time, stirring until each addition is absorbed into the rice. Continue adding stock in this way, cooking until the rice is creamy but the grains are still firm. This should take about 20 minutes.
4. Return the lamb and almonds to the pan and add the apricots and coriander. Mix, season to taste with salt and pepper and cook for 1 minute. Cover and leave the risotto to rest for a few minutes before serving.

Serves 4/ Preparation time: 10 minutes/ Cooking time: 30 minutes

Wafered Lamb and Mint Risotto

425 g/14 oz lean lamb fillet, very thinly sliced

50 g/2 oz butter

2 tablespoons olive oil

1 large onion, chopped

3 garlic cloves, chopped

375 g/12 oz risotto rice

150 ml/¼ pint white wine

1.2 litres/2 pints hot Vegetable Stock
   (see page 19)

100 g/3½ oz sugar snap peas, sliced lengthways

small handful of mint sprigs, roughly chopped

50 g/2 oz Parmesan cheese, freshly grated

salt and pepper

1. Trim any fat from the lamb and season with salt and pepper. Melt the butter with the oil in a large, heavy-based saucepan. Add the lamb and cook, stirring frequently, for about 5 minutes, until browned. Remove the lamb and set aside.

2. Add the onion to the pan and sauté gently for 5 minutes until softened. Add the garlic and rice and stir well to coat the grains with the butter and oil. Add the wine, bring to the boil and cook, stirring until almost all the liquid has evaporated.

3. Add the hot stock, a large ladleful at a time, stirring until each addition is absorbed into the rice. Continue adding stock in this way, cooking until the rice is creamy but the grains are still firm. This should take about 20 minutes.

4. Return the lamb to the pan with the sugar snap peas and mint, and season to taste with salt and pepper. Cook for 1 minute, stirring. Stir in the Parmesan, cover and leave the risotto to rest for a few minutes before serving.

Serves 4/ Preparation time: 10–15 minutes, plus cooling/ Cooking time: 35 minutes

Chicken and Watercress Risotto Cakes

250 g/8 oz skinless, boneless chicken breasts

50 g/2 oz butter

1 onion, chopped

4 garlic cloves, crushed

200 g/7 oz risotto rice

600 ml/1 pint hot Chicken or Vegetable Stock
 (see pages 17 and 19)

75 g/3 oz Parmesan cheese, freshly grated

75 g/3 oz watercress, tough stalks removed

1 egg, lightly beaten

flour, for dusting

75 g/3 oz polenta

vegetable oil, for shallow-frying

salad, to serve

1. Finely chop the chicken. Melt the butter in a large, heavy-based saucepan. Add the chicken and cook, stirring frequently, for 2–3 minutes, until cooked through. Remove with a slotted spoon and set aside.

2. Add the onion to the pan and sauté gently for 5 minutes. Add the garlic and rice and stir well to coat the grains with the butter. Add the hot stock, a large ladleful at a time, stirring until each addition is absorbed into the rice. Continue adding stock in this way, cooking until the rice is creamy but the grains are still firm. This should take about 20 minutes. Stir in the Parmesan.

3. Roughly chop the watercress and add to the pan, stirring until it has wilted. Add the cooked chicken and season to taste with salt and pepper. Remove the pan from the heat and leave to cool.

4. Put the beaten egg on a plate. Put the polenta on another plate. Using lightly floured hands, shape the risotto mixture into 8 even-sized pieces. Flatten into cakes and coat first in the beaten egg, then in the polenta.

5. Heat a little vegetable oil in a large frying pan and fry the cakes for about 3 minutes on each side until golden. Drain on kitchen paper and serve with salad.

Spicy Chicken and Broccoli Risotto

40 g/1½ oz butter

2 tablespoons olive oil

2 skinless, boneless chicken breasts, diced

½ onion, very finely chopped

1 garlic clove, finely chopped

1–2 fresh red chillies, deseeded and very finely chopped

300 g/10 oz risotto rice

1 litre/1¾ pints hot Chicken Stock (see page 17)

250 g/8 oz broccoli florets

3 tablespoons freshly grated Parmesan cheese

salt and pepper

1. Melt 15 g/½ oz of the butter with the oil in a heavy-based saucepan. Add the diced chicken and sauté gently for 2–3 minutes. Add the onion and sauté for 5 minutes, until softened but not coloured. Add the garlic and chilli and cook until the garlic is golden.

2. Add the rice to the pan and stir well to coat the grains with the butter and oil. Add the hot stock, a large ladleful at a time, stirring until each addition is absorbed into the rice. Continue adding stock in this way, cooking until the rice is creamy but the grains are still firm. This should take about 20 minutes.

3. Plunge the broccoli florets into a pan of boiling water for 1 minute. Drain thoroughly and add to the rice with the Parmesan. Season to taste with salt and pepper and stir in the remaining butter. Cover and leave the risotto to rest for a few minutes before serving.

Serves 4/ Preparation time: 15–20 minutes/ Cooking time: 30 minutes

Chicken Liver Risotto

This recipe cheats a little, but it much more convenient and less time-consuming than an authentic risotto cooked in the traditional way – and it works very well.

2 tablespoons extra virgin olive oil

1 onion, finely chopped

250 g/8 oz chicken livers, cores removed, roughly chopped

1 garlic clove, crushed

300 g/10 oz risotto rice

125 ml/4 fl oz dry white wine

about 1 litre/1¾ pints hot Chicken Stock (see page 17)

large pinch of saffron threads

125 g/4 oz frozen peas or petits pois

6 tablespoons double cream

2 tablespoons chopped flat leaf parsley (optional)

about 50 g/2 oz Parmesan cheese, thinly shaved

salt and pepper

1. Heat the olive oil in a large flameproof casserole. Add the onion and sauté over a low heat, stirring frequently, for about 5 minutes, until softened but not coloured.
2. Add the chicken livers and the crushed garlic, increase the heat to moderate and cook, stirring constantly, for 2–3 minutes, or until the livers change colour on all sides.
3. Add the rice and stir well to coat the grains with the oil. Add the wine and stir until the bubbles subside.
4. Pour in 600 ml/1 pint of the hot stock, add the saffron, season to taste with salt and pepper and stir well. Bring to the boil, then cover and simmer over a gentle heat for 10 minutes, stirring occasionally to prevent the rice from sticking to the bottom of the pan.
5. Add a further 400 ml/14 fl oz hot stock to the risotto, stir well to combine, then add the peas. Cover and simmer for a further 10 minutes, stirring occasionally and adding a little more stock if necessary.
6. Remove the pan from the heat and gently fold in the cream and the parsley, if using. Adjust the seasoning to taste. Serve hot, topped with Parmesan shavings.

Serves 6/ Preparation time: 35 minutes/ Cooking time: 2 hours

Chicken Risotto with White Wine and Tomatoes

Every part of a whole chicken is used in this hearty risotto – as you make the stock before you start to cook the rest of the dish.

1 kg/2 lb oven-ready chicken

2 litres/3½ pints water

2 celery sticks

2 onions

2 carrots

3–4 tablespoons olive oil

7 tablespoons white wine

375 g/12 oz tomatoes, skinned and mashed

500 g/1 lb risotto rice

75 g/3 oz butter, softened

75 g/3 oz Parmesan cheese, freshly grated

salt and pepper

1–2 tablespoons chopped parsley, to garnish

1. Remove the bones from the chicken and place them in a large pan with the water. Add 1 celery stick, 1 onion and 1 carrot and season with salt and pepper. Bring to the boil, lower the heat, cover and simmer for 1½ hours. Strain the stock and keep hot.

2. Meanwhile, dice the chicken meat, removing and discarding all the skin. Finely chop the remaining celery, onion and carrot. Heat the olive oil, add the chopped vegetables and sauté until lightly coloured. Add the chicken and cook, stirring constantly, for a further 5 minutes. Add the wine, bring to the boil and cook, stirring, until it has evaporated.

3. Add the tomatoes and season to taste with salt and pepper. Cover and cook over a low heat for 20 minutes, adding a little of the hot chicken stock if the mixture becomes dry.

4. Add the rice. Add the hot stock, a large ladleful at a time, stirring until each addition is absorbed into the rice. Continue adding stock in this way, cooking until the rice is creamy but the grains are still firm. This should take about 20 minutes.

5. Remove from the heat, add the butter and Parmesan and fold in gently. Cover and leave the risotto to rest for a few minutes before serving, sprinkled with parsley.

4 Desserts

Serves 4/ Preparation time: 5 minutes/ Cooking time: 30 minutes

Venetian Rice Pudding

75 g/3 oz sultanas

3 tablespoons medium sherry (optional)

600 ml/1 pint hot semi-skimmed milk

150 ml/¼ pint double cream

1 vanilla pod, split lengthways, or 2 teaspoons
   vanilla essence

50 g/2 oz caster sugar

½ teaspoon ground mixed spice

finely grated rind of 1 lemon

125 g/4 oz risotto rice

lemon rind strips, to decorate

**This will be a revelation for anyone whose only experience with rice pudding
was during lunches at school.**

1. Put the sultanas in a bowl with the sherry, if using, and leave to soak while you
   make the risotto. Put the milk in a saucepan with the cream, vanilla pod or
   essence, sugar, spice and lemon rind and bring almost to the boil.

2. Add the rice and cook on the lowest heat, stirring frequently for 20–30 minutes or
   until the rice is creamy but the grains are still firm.

3. Stir in the sultanas and any sherry from the bowl and serve warm or cold
   decorated with lemon rind strips.

Serves 4/ Preparation time: 5 minutes, plus cooling/ Cooking time: 45–55 minutes

Iced Fig Risotto

This is the perfect dessert to serve at the end of a leisurely supper on a warm summer evening.

600 ml/1 pint semi-skimmed milk

40 g/1½ oz caster sugar

finely grated rind of 1 orange

125 g/4 oz risotto rice

butter, for greasing

8 fresh figs

2 tablespoons clear honey

2 tablespoons orange juice

200 g/7 oz vanilla ice-cream

1. Put the milk, sugar and orange rind in a large saucepan and bring almost to the boil. Add the rice and cook on the lowest possible heat, stirring frequently, for 25–35 minutes or until the rice is creamy but the grains are still firm. Remove from the heat and set aside to cool.

2. Halve the figs and place in a lightly buttered shallow ovenproof dish. Drizzle with the honey and orange juice and bake in a preheated oven, 200ºC (400ºF), Gas Mark 6, for about 20 minutes, or until beginning to colour.

3. Scoop the ice-cream into the rice mixture and stir until it has just melted to make a creamy sauce. Spoon into bowls with the figs and cooking juices and serve immediately.

Strawberry Risotto

250 g/8 oz small strawberries

2 tablespoons orange-flavoured liqueur
  (optional)

50 g/2 oz caster sugar, plus 2 tablespoons

500 ml/17 fl oz semi-skimmed milk

25 g/1 oz unsalted butter

100 g/3½ oz risotto rice

mint sprigs, to decorate

1. Thinly slice the strawberries and put them in a bowl with the orange-flavoured liqueur, if using, and 2 tablespoons sugar. Bring the milk almost to the boil in a saucepan with the remaining sugar.

2. Melt the butter in a large heavy-based saucepan. Add the rice and stir well to coat the grains with the butter. Pour the hot milk over the rice and cook gently on the lowest possible heat, stirring frequently, for about 25–35 minutes or until the rice is creamy but the grains are still firm.

3. Lightly fold the strawberries and juices into the risotto and serve immediately, decorated with mint sprigs.

Blueberry and Vanilla Risotto

Rich and creamy, this fruity dessert is irresistible.

600 ml/1 pint hot semi-skimmed milk

50 g/2 oz golden caster sugar, plus 1 tablespoon

2 teaspoons vanilla essence

40 g/1½ oz unsalted butter

125 g/4 oz risotto rice

150 g/5 oz fresh blueberries

4 tablespoons double cream

shortbread or dessert biscuits, to serve
  (optional)

1. Put the milk in a saucepan with 50 g/2 oz of the sugar and the vanilla and bring almost to the boil.
2. Meanwhile, melt the butter in a large, heavy-based saucepan. Add the rice and stir well to coat the grains with the butter. Add the hot milk and bring to the boil. Reduce the heat and simmer, stirring frequently, for 25–35 minutes or until the rice is creamy, but the grains are still firm.
3. Gently stir the blueberries into the risotto and spoon into bowls. Spoon over the cream and sprinkle with the remaining sugar. Serve with shortbread or dessert biscuits, if liked.

Mascarpone Risotto with Roasted Peaches

Peaches and creamy mascarpone cheese are a classic combination, but you could use nectarines, if you prefer.

600 ml/1 pint semi-skimmed milk

50 g/2 oz caster sugar

15 g/½ oz unsalted butter, melted

1 tablespoon icing sugar

3 ripe peaches, thickly sliced

125 g/4 oz risotto rice

125 g/4 oz mascarpone cheese

2 tablespoons medium sherry

50 g/2 oz amaretti or ratafia biscuits, lightly crushed (optional)

1. Put the milk in a saucepan with the sugar and bring almost to the boil.

2. Meanwhile, brush the peaches with the melted butter, sprinkle with icing sugar and cook under a preheated grill until they are beginning to turn golden brown.

3. Add the rice to the hot milk, bring to the boil and then simmer gently, stirring frequently, for 25–35 minutes or until the rice is creamy but the grains are still firm. Stir in the mascarpone until melted, then stir in the sherry.

4. Spoon the risotto into bowls and top with the peaches. Serve sprinkled with the crushed biscuits, if liked.

Baked Cherry Risotto

500 ml/17 fl oz semi-skimmed milk

125 g/4 oz caster sugar

1 teaspoon vanilla essence

100 g/3½ fl oz risotto rice

150 ml/¼ pint double cream

400 g/13 oz fresh cherries, pitted and halved

1. Put the milk in a large, heavy-based saucepan with 50 g/2 oz of the sugar and the vanilla essence. Bring just to the boil. Add the rice, reduce the heat and simmer very gently, stirring frequently, for 25–35 minutes or until the rice is creamy but the grains are still firm. Remove from the heat and stir in the cream.

2. Scatter the cherries in a 900 ml/1½ pint shallow ovenproof dish or individual ovenproof dishes. Spoon the risotto over the cherries, spreading it to the edges of the dish.

3. Sprinkle with the remaining sugar and cook under a preheated grill for 4–5 minutes until the sugar has caramelized. Leave to cool slightly before serving.

Dessert Wine Risotto with Florentine Brittle

50 g/2 oz golden caster sugar

450 ml/¾ pint water

1 cinnamon stick, halved

300 ml/½ pint sweet dessert wine

125 g/4 oz risotto rice

3 tablespoons double cream

FLORENTINE BRITTLE:

vegetable oil, for brushing

25 g/1 oz unsalted butter

25 g/1 oz caster sugar

25 g/1 oz flaked almonds

2 tablespoons raisins

3 glacé cherries, chopped

1 teaspoon plain flour

1. First make the brittle. Lightly oil a baking sheet. Melt the butter in a small saucepan, then stir in the sugar until dissolved. Add the remaining brittle ingredients and stir well. Spoon on to the prepared baking sheet and spread very thinly.

2. Bake in a preheated oven, 180°C (350°F), Gas Mark 4, for 15–20 minutes until deep golden. Remove from the oven and leave on the baking sheet until cool. Lift from the sheet and transfer to a plate.

3. Meanwhile, make the risotto. Put the sugar in a large, heavy-based saucepan with the water and heat until the sugar dissolves. Add the cinnamon stick, wine and rice. Bring to the boil, reduce the heat and simmer gently, stirring frequently, for 25–35 minutes or until the rice is creamy but the grains are still firm.

4. Stir the cream into the risotto and spoon into dishes. Break the Florentine brittle into pieces and scatter over the risotto before serving.

Spiced Risotto Cakes with Plum Compôte

Contrasting colours and textures make a simple dessert into a work of art.

500 ml/17 fl oz milk

50 g/2 oz caster sugar

½ teaspoon ground cinnamon

freshly grated nutmeg

125 g/4 oz risotto rice

1 egg, lightly beaten

75 g/3 oz amaretti biscuits, crushed

plain flour, for dusting

vegetable oil, for frying

mint sprigs, to decorate

lightly whipped cream or crème fraîche,
    to serve (optional)

COMPOTE:

50 g/2 oz caster sugar

300 ml/½ pint water

finely grated rind and juice of 1 lemon

500 g/1 lb plums, halved

1. To make the risotto cakes, put the milk in a large, heavy-based saucepan with the sugar, cinnamon and nutmeg, and bring almost to the boil. Add the rice, reduce the heat to its lowest setting and simmer gently, stirring frequently, for about 25–35 minutes or until the rice is creamy but the grains are still firm. Remove from the heat and set aside to cool.

2. Meanwhile, to make the compôte, put the sugar in a saucepan with the water and heat gently until the sugar dissolves. Add the lemon rind and juice and the plums and simmer gently for about 10 minutes, until the plums are tender.

3. Put the beaten egg on a plate and the crushed biscuits on another. When the risotto is cool enough to handle, shape it into 8 small cakes using lightly floured hands. Coat first in the beaten egg and then in the biscuit crumbs.

4. Heat a 5 ml/¼ inch depth of oil in a frying pan and fry the risotto cakes very gently for 1–2 minutes on each side, until golden. Drain on kitchen paper and serve with the compôte, decorated with mint sprigs and accompanied by lightly whipped cream or crème fraîche, if liked.

Chocolate Risotto

When you are adding the chocolate to this dessert, try not to over-mix it, as the marbled effect looks good.

600 ml/1 pint milk

25 g/1 oz sugar

50 g/2 oz butter

125 g/4 oz risotto rice

50 g/2 oz hazelnuts, toasted and chopped

50 g/2 oz sultanas

125 g/4 oz good quality dark chocolate, grated

splash of brandy (optional)

grated chocolate, to decorate

1. Put the milk and sugar into a saucepan and heat until almost boiling.
2. Melt the butter in a heavy-based saucepan, add the rice and stir well to coat the grains with the butter.
3. Add the hot milk, a large ladleful at a time, stirring until each addition is absorbed into the rice. Continue adding milk in this way, cooking until the rice is creamy but the grains are still firm. This should take about 25–35 minutes.
4. Finally, add the hazelnuts, sultanas, grated chocolate and a splash of brandy, if using, and mix quickly. Serve decorated with grated chocolate.

Index

Acknowledgements

Senior Editor: Sarah Ford
Senior Designer: Joanna Bennett
Production Controller: Viv Cracknell

Special Photography: William Reavell
Food Stylist: Oona van den Berg

All other photography Octopus Publishing
Group Limited/ David Loftus 23, 39, 42, 109 top
right/ Hilary Moore 104/ Ian Wallace front cover
centre, front cover bottom right, 21 bottom centre,
26, 29, 30, 31, 33, 37, 41, 45, 48, 59, 78–79, 96/
Philip Webb 56, 57/ Sandra Lane 92/